12,99

PONS

Wolfgang Hohlbein
Dream of Dragons

PONS GmbH
Stuttgart

PONS

Wolfgang Hohlbein
Dream of Dragons

Englisch von Brian Melican

1. Auflage 2011

PONS Produktinfos und Shop: www.pons.de
PONS Sprachenportal: www.pons.eu
E-Mail: info@pons.de

Englische Übersetzung, Annotationen und Übungen: Brian Melican
Redaktion: Jill Williams
Projektmanagement: Mareike Geib
Logoentwicklung: Erwin Poell, Heidelberg
Logoüberarbeitung: Sabine Redlin, Ludwigsburg
Sprecher/Tonaufnahmen: Dave Hickman, UK
Layout: Petra Michel Gestaltung & Typografie, Bamberg
Satz: Satzkasten, Dollenbacher & Müller, Stuttgart
Coverillustration und Einbandgestaltung: hilden_design, München
Druck und Bindung: Print Consult GmbH, Oettingenstraße 23, München

Printed in Czech Republic.
ISBN 978-3-12-010071-3

Inhaltsangabe

Überglücklich kehrte Timucin mit seiner Braut Arbesa nach fast einem Jahr Abwesenheit voller Tatendrang nach Hause zu seinem Klan zurück. Doch sein Vater war entführt worden und Timucin musste die Führung des Klans übernehmen, geleitet vom Rat seines geheimnisvollen Drachens.

Nun ist er auf einer halsbrecherischen Flucht, ohne Freunde und Kampfgefährten, nur mit Arbesa und seiner Mutter als letzten Rückhalt. Und ihre Feine rücken immer näher. Im eiskalten Winter der Steppe hat er nur ein Ziel vor Augen: er muss den Heiligen Berg erreichen und dort die rettende Hilfe finden.

Da bekommen sie Hilfe: Timucins Schwurbruder Chuzir hat sie auf ihrem Irrweg eingeholt und will sie vor den heranrückenden Feinden schützen. Timucin lässt Arbesa und seine Mutter in Chuzirs Obhut zurück, um den Heiligen Berg zu besteigen – doch dies erweist sich als großer Fehler. Timucin gerät in Gefangenschaft! Kann er seinen grausamen Wärtern entkommen?

Auftretende Personen

Timucin, der junge Dschingis Khan
Timucin ist ein junger Krieger des Kijat-Klans und sollte sich eigentlich auf seine späteren Aufgaben als Khan des Klans vorbereiten. Doch sein Stamm ist in alle Himmelsrichtungen zersprengt, er selbst ist auf der Flucht und muss nun seine Fähigkeiten als Krieger unter Beweis stellen. Sein Name wird *Timudschin* ausgesprochen.

Arbesa, Timucins Braut
Arbesa ist Timucins Verlobte, obwohl sie beide noch ziemlich jung sind. Doch so ist es Brauch in ihren Klans. Sie stichelt gerne und ist vorlaut, doch gleichzeitig ist sie ein herzensguter Mensch.

Üdschin, Timucins Mutter
Üdschin ist Timucins Mutter und eine sehr stolze Frau, die typische tüchtige Ehefrau eines Steppenkriegers. Obwohl sie schon älter und krank ist, versucht sie, sich nicht anmerken zu lassen, dass die Strapazen der Flucht sie sehr mitnehmen.

Chuzir, Timucins Schwurbruder
Chuzir ist Timucins bester Freund und Schwurbruder. Er ist ein hervorragender junger Krieger und war in vielen schwierigen Situationen schon Timucins größte Stütze. Auch jetzt versucht er, Timucin aus seiner Notlage zu befreien. Sein Name wird *Tschusir* ausgesprochen.

Sarantuya, Timucins Drache
Timucins Traumdrache Sarantuya ist seine beste Ratgeberin und führt ihn weise. Sie ist der letzte Drache, der mit einem Menschen von Timucins Klan die ewige Partnerschaft eingegangen ist. Denn die Menschen sind zu oft habgierig und gewalttätig, die Drachen dagegen verabscheuen Gewalt.
Ob Timucin ihre Partnerschaft erhalten kann?

WOLFGANG HOHLBEIN

DREAM OF DRAGONS

Forced to Flee

TR. 01

He has not been able to save his father. Nor has he married Arbesa, to whom he has been engaged for so long. And the clan over which he rules[1] is, in all truth, now little more than a handful of scattered[2] survivors. They have fled in every direction and are forced to beg[3] for food and shelter[4] since they are too weak and too afraid to steal it. Bajar and Batu, his two dogs, are dead. They were quite possibly the only true friends he has ever had. They died in one of the countless[5] battles that have, ever since that fateful[6] day, dominated his life like the rising and setting of the sun. More and more, he is asking himself if they will ever stop.

The purse[7] on his belt, light enough before, has been empty for two days now. There is no money left, and now he will have to either steal or beg to get his next meal if he cannot hunt it himself. The last time they were forced to flee so hastily[8], they had to leave most of their belongings[9] behind and so they do not even have a yurt[10] to protect them from the cold of the night. There are only two arrows[11] left in his quiver[12] – well, three, but he would rather starve than shoot the third arrow, this most special of arrows. They haven't had any fresh water for the past two days, since his mother Üdschin caught a fever. Although she is like all women of the tribe and would never allow herself to complain, Timucin can tell that her condition is getting worse and that she is coming to the end of her strength. So this is the situation in which he, Khan of the Kijat tribe,

1 **to rule** – *herrschen*
2 **scattered** – *zerstreut, versprengt*
3 **to beg** – *betteln*
4 **shelter** – *Obdach*
5 **countless** – *zahllos*
6 **fateful** – *schicksalhaft*
7 **purse** – *Geldbeutel*
8 **to flee hastily** – *hastig fliehen*
9 **belongings** – *Habe*
10 **yurt** – *Jurte (Zelt)*
11 **arrow** – *Pfeil*
12 **quiver** – *Köcher*

now finds himself. Unless he is forgetting any other disastrous circumstances[1], of course.

Üdschin's pony has been lamed[2] on the front foot, but you can't bring yourself to kill it, although you know you must.

"Yes, and at least we'll have some meat!" Although only he can hear Sarantuya's voice in his thoughts, and despite the fact that she will understand an unspoken reply as well, he speaks out loud. He has got into the habit[3], although he doesn't remember when or why any more. He does know that Arbesa doesn't like him doing it, though, since she is afraid that other members of the tribe will think he has gone mad if they hear him talking to himself.

Sarantuya, however, doesn't seem to mind, and it is quite possible that he is the only member of the Kijat tribe left alive. Apart from his mother, of course.

Are you feeling sorry for yourself again, my Khan? asks the dragon in his thoughts.

Timucin forbids[4] himself from answering this question. Before, Sarantuya had only ever spoken to him in his dreams, but since they have started out[5] for the Holy[6] Mountain, she has been talking more and more often. She now speaks to him when he is awake, and her tone has changed. She is still the big, gentle[7] dragon he has always known since his earliest childhood, since she first appeared to him in his dreams, and despite her monstrous size and awesome[8] power, she is always willing to have a laugh. Or at least laugh at him. Yet she sounds different now, although he can't quite put his finger on it, as if she is worried about something that has happened (or will happen) without Timucin knowing it.

1 **disastrous circumstances** – *desaströse Umstände*
2 **to lame** – *lahmen*
3 **to get into the habit of doing sth.** – *sich angewöhnen, etw. zu tun*
4 **to forbid** – *verbieten*
5 **to start out** – *sich auf den Weg machen*
6 **holy** – *heilig*
7 **gentle** – *sanftmütig*
8 **awesome** – *Ehrfucht gebietend*

This is a disturbing[1] thought. What is even more disturbing, however, is that the dragon doesn't reply to it, not even with a scornful[2] remark. Before, she never missed a chance to jibe[3] at him.

He heard the sound of feet upon stones, and snow starts to fall from the bush behind which they have been sheltering from the chilling[4] wind. Suddenly, a sleek[5] figure in a thick fur coat[6] breaks through. Although he is not yet fully grown and will certainly never be one of the tallest, this person only just reaches his chin[7]. The fur cap covering her head of raven-black hair does not even reach his forehead. From looking at her, he can see that she is so cold that she can barely move. Each time she breathes out, her face disappears behind a thick white cloud. She looks so small and delicate, Timucin feels sad and guilty[8], yet at the same time, just the sight of her fills his heart with warmth. It makes it easier for him to endure[9] exhaustion[10] and pain.

"Where were you?" he asks.

Arbesa nods to the pile of wood behind her and she crouches down[11] to the fire to rub her hands together over the flame. The small amount of wood that she has managed to find will not be enough to make a big fire, and this has advantages, because fire means smoke and smoke makes it difficult to stay hidden from enemies. The cold, however, is a powerful enemy in itself. Winter has come early this year and promises to be especially cold.

"What did you do there?"

1 **disturbing** – *verstörend*
2 **scornful** – *spöttisch*
3 **to jibe at sb.** – *jdn. foppen*
4 **chilling** – *schneidend, eisig*
5 **sleek** – *schmal*
6 **fur coat** – *Pelzmantel*
7 **this person only just reaches his chin** – *die Person reicht ihm gerade bis zum Kinn*
8 **guilty** – *schuldig*
9 **to endure** – *ertragen*
10 **exhaustion** – *Erschöpfung*
11 **to crouch down** – *in die Hocke gehen*

Arbesa lowers her fingers right down to the fire until they are almost burning and then looks up at him reproachfully[1] from under the rim[2] of her straggly[3] fur cap.

"That is an impolite question to ask," she replies after a moment's hesitation. Timucin thinks about this for a while and only understands its meaning as he hears a humorous[4], sneering[5] laugh somewhere at the back of his mind. Then he feels his ears getting red, again.

"Oh", he murmurs[6].

Arbesa is discreet enough to leave it at[7] a quiet laugh, and then beckons him to sit next to her[8]. He obeys silently, still a little embarrassed. His face starts to burn slightly as he leans over the fire, but the warmth coming from Arbesa as he sits next to her has a far greater effect, even if this is only because she and his mother are the only two things he has left. He is ashamed of thinking this the moment after he has thought it.

"How long do you think we will need?" she asks after they have sat next to each other in silence for a while. Timucin looks to the west, where a blurred[9] shadow is rising against the dawn[10]. It is the same shadow that they have been using to find their way for more than a week now, perhaps for two. The longer their desperate flight lasts, the more he is starting to lose his hold on time. At times, it is as if only a few hours have passed since he looked into Arbesa's bottomless[11] black eyes. At others, it seems like years.

In a way, it is both, little Khan, whispers[12] the dragon in his mind. It sounds absurd, but Sarantuya keeps going: *You'll soon understand what I mean, little Khan,* she continues.

1 **reproachfully** – *vorwurfsvoll*
2 **rim** – *Rand*
3 **straggly** – *struppig*
4 **humorous** – *gutmütig, humorvoll*
5 **sneering** – *spöttisch*
6 **to murmur** – *murmeln*
7 **to leave it at sth.** – *es bei etw. belassen*
8 **she beckons him to sit next to her** – *sie macht eine einladende Geste neben sich*
9 **blurred** – *verschwommen*
10 **dawn** – *Morgendämmerung*
11 **bottomless** – *unergründlich*
12 **to whisper** – *flüstern*

Don't call me that! he thinks angrily. Out loud, he says: "Two days."

Arbesa nods. The yellow flames are licking at her fingers and reach them now and again, yet if she feels any pain at all, she is not showing it. She doesn't say that he already said "two days" two days ago either, and that he will probably say "two days" in two days' time, too, if they haven't reached the Holy Mountain by then. She doesn't ask him why they are headed for[1] this cold, isolated[2] place, to Burchan Chaldun. She hasn't once asked him since they began this hopeless[3] march, and Timucin is silently thankful that she hasn't, because he couldn't answer her if she did.

Perhaps there is no reason why they are going there, he thinks. Perhaps any place was as good as the next. He has no home, no tribesmen[4] and no friends to whom they can turn[5].

Arbesa takes his hand. Her slender[6] fingers are as cold as ice and very fragile[7]. Yet they fill him with a warmth so strong that it is difficult for him not to reach out and pull her to him.

What would he do without her? He asks himself this question and answers it immediately: nothing. It is that simple, because without her, he would be long dead by now[8].

"Üdschin is sick," she says suddenly. She sounds sad.

"I know," he answers, "and her horse is lame."

Arbesa nods. She would have to be blind not to notice this, not to notice just how hard it has been for the poor creature to drag itself along[9] today. It was barely able to pull its own

DRACHENFRAGE

Where does Timucin tell his mother and Arbesa that they are fleeing to?

1 **to be headed for sth.** – *zu einem Ort unterwegs sein*
2 **isolated** – *fern, isoliert*
3 **hopeless** – *hoffnungslos, aussichtslos*
4 **tribesmen** – *Stammesmänner*
5 **to whom they can turn** – *an die sie sich wenden können*
6 **slender** – *schmal*
7 **fragile** – *zerbrechlich*
8 **he would be long dead by now** – *er wäre jetzt schon lange nicht mehr am Leben*
9 **to drag oneself along** – *sich dahinschleppen*

weight, let alone that of Timucin's mother, who is hardly bigger than a child.

Arbesa is silent. She does not voice a word[1] of doubt or criticism, and she has not done over the past months, despite all the mistakes that he has made. And there have been plenty[2] of mistakes.

"I'm going to have to kill the pony," he says after a while, "and end its suffering[3]."

"And your mother needs the meat," said Arbesa in agreement. Timucin waits for Sarantuya to say something, probably to tell him he is wrong, but the dragon remains silent. The wind is louder for a second, as if to mock him[4], driving another flurry[5] of snowflakes off the bush. The snow settles slowly on Arbesa, himself and his mother, sleeping on the other side of the fire. It is almost unearthly[6] how slowly it falls. Perhaps it is because here, deep in the desert, there is no real snow, but just frozen powder mixed with dew[7]. This is worse, however, because this freezing powder creeps in[8] everywhere, under clothes, into the body, and takes the cold with it. It is as if it is sucking the last warmth out of his limbs[9], out of his bones.

One of the animals is snorting[10] pathetically[11]. It is the injured horse; Timucin knows it without even looking. He can feel its pain.

"Go on, put the poor thing out of its misery[12]. Üdschin can take my horse. I'm young, I'll be fine on foot."

1 **to voice a word** – *ein Wort verlieren*
2 **plenty** – *genug, reichlich*
3 **to suffer** – *leiden*
4 **as if to mock him** – *wie um ihn zu verspotten*
5 **flurry** – *Gestöber*
6 **unearthly** – *unheimlich*
7 **dew** – *Tau*
8 **to creep in** – *hineinschleichen*
9 **limb** – *Glied*
10 **to snort** – *schnauben*
11 **pathetic** – *jämmerlich*
12 **to put sb. / sth. out of its misery** – *jds. Leiden ein Ende setzen*

Yes, of course, thought Timucin. Her little feet are probably bleeding in her fur-lined[1] boots. I'll go on foot. And that's the end of the matter[2]! Nevertheless, her readiness to offer her horse fills his heart with warmth.

He stands up and goes to the horses. The pony is snorting quietly and he avoids its gaze[3] as it looks up at him. Although he thinks he is being stupid, he has an idea that the pony knows what is coming.

It knows, whispers the dragon in his thoughts, but it isn't angry at you. It's not your fault that it fell over. It is in pain and knows that the pain will not stop.

Sarantuya is telling the truth, he knows this. However, he still cannot hold the animal's gaze as he removes its harness[4] and the blanket. He whispers to it, meaningless[5] but comforting[6] words, as he tries to take his knife from his belt as quietly as he can. Suddenly, as quickly as lightning, he slits the pony's throat[7].

The pony doesn't make a sound, but collapses as if it has been struck by lightning[8]. He and Arbesa cut the best bits straight from the body and eat them raw and warm just to still the worst of their hunger. They use the last of their salt to preserve[9] as much of the meat as they can carry and then Arbesa stokes[10] the flames and they grill as much as they can of what is left. They eat more than ten hungry men could normally stomach[11], and yet still Timucin sees that they will be forced to leave behind far more meat than they can use, and he is disgusted by this[12] thought. He is from a tribe that lived a hard life on the steppe, a life full of privations[13] that has taught him

1 **fur-lined** – *pelzgefüttert*
2 **and that's the end of the matter! (Redewendung)** – *und Schluss!*
3 **to avoid sb.'s gaze** – *jdns. Blick ausweichen*
4 **harness** – *Zaumzeug*
5 **meaningless** – *bedeutungslos, sinnlos*
6 **comforting** – *beruhigend*
7 **to slit sb.'s throat** – *jdm. die Kehle durchschneiden*
8 **as if it has been struck by lighting** – *wie vom Blitz getroffen*
9 **to preserve** – *haltbar machen*
10 **to stoke** – *anfachen*
11 **to stomach sth.** – *etw. verkraften*
12 **he is disgusted by it** – *es ist ihm tiefst zuwider*
13 **full of privations (altertümlich)** – *reich an Entbehrungen*

never to waste anything. Furthermore, he feels as if he is being unjust[1] to the animal by turning down the last gift[2] it was able to make him.

The smell of grilled meat wakes his mother, who looks worse than the evening before. Just reaching out to take the meat that Arbesa has speared on a stick[3] clearly takes a huge effort. Üdschin refuses help[4] without a word, for she is a proud woman above all.

They take their time and eat slowly, eating only as much as they can without feeling ill. They start to feel sleepy, but Timucin does not give in to[5] it. He puts out the fire and starts to load the few belongings they still have onto the two remaining horses. Üdschin watches him silently, but as he extends his hand to her, she takes a step back and shakes her head.

"We only have two horses left," she says, "and there are three of us. You'll have to leave me behind."

"It'll be the death of you!" replies Timucin.

"It'll be the death of both of you if you don't!" she says, quietly but firmly. "The Tajin are still following us, and you know them well. You know that they will not give up[6]. Then they will take all three of us prisoner."

Timucin wishes he could tell her she is wrong, but he can't, because she is right. They have been almost ceaselessly[7] on the run[8] since that fateful day ten months ago when the warriors of the enemy tribe attacked their village, killed half of the men and sent the other half fleeing. All this time, the Tajin spies have not once lost their trail[9]. They have been catching up[10] for some days now, not quickly, but consistently[11]. Timucin

1 **unjust** – *unfair*
2 **gift** – *Geschenk*
3 **to spear on a stick** – *auf einem Stock spießen*
4 **to refuse help** – *Hilfe ablehnen*
5 **to give in to sth.** – *etw. zulassen*
6 **to give up** – *aufgeben*
7 **ceaselessly** – *ohne Unterbrechung*
8 **on the run** – *auf der Flucht*
9 **trail** – *Spur*
10 **to catch up** – *aufholen*
11 **consistently** – *beharrlich*

has tried to hide this from the women, but he can tell that he has not been able to, even if neither Arbesa nor his mother have said anything about it until now. The Tajin were catching up, and they would catch up even faster if Timucin slowed down.

Despite this, however, there could be the possibility of leaving his mother behind. He might just as well[1] take a knife and cut her throat, which would be a form of mercy[2] compared with what will happen to her if she falls into the hands of the Tajin. Although his mother is an old woman, forty years old at least, this will not protect her from their cruelty[3]. Age will be no shield for Üdschin.

Arbesa is the one who settles things in the way only she knows how.

"What rubbish," she says, "Timucin and I will take turns walking[4]. We'll probably be even quicker than with the lame horse." She gestures to Timucin and orders him to help his mother onto the horse: "There's no time to lose!"

1 **he might just as well...** – *er könnte genauso gut...*
2 **mercy** – *Gnade*
3 **cruelty** – *Grausamkeit*
4 **to take turns doing sth.** – *etw. abwechselnd machen*

A Familiar Face

TR. 02

The following morning does not bring them any closer to the Holy Mountain. It brings nothing except colder weather and an even higher fever for Üdschin. You can see how ill she is, and smell it, too. Since she was born, Üdschin has always been a very clean woman, but now she smells of sickness and fever. Despite the fact she is suffering thirst and icy cold, Timucin knows that the thing that is causing her more pain than anything else is the shame of being ill.

As they stop to rest at midday, and to eat the rest of the grilled meat from the day before, he casually[1] takes her knife and forgets to give it back.

After resting, they set off again and do not stop until long after sundown, where they find shelter under an even more pathetic bush than the last time. He lies close to Arbesa so that they can share the warmth of their bodies, but does not touch her. He stays awake despite his efforts to force himself to go to sleep. Of course, this keeps him awake for even longer.

When he finally does get to sleep, the dragon does not come, so he wakes up long before sunrise next to the fire, which has burned down. A feeling of being lost and lonely grips his heart like an icy fist.

It is too cold, even for this hour of day, and too quiet, even for this, the loneliest place in the world.

Does he feel this only because Sarantuya has not come? While he waits for the sun to come up, he asks himself (not for the first time, but the first time so seriously) if he ever really did have a dream-dragon? He has known the dragon for as long as he can remember, and he is quite sure that Sarantuya used to visit him every night. They used to chat, she would play jokes on him[2]. Sometimes she would offer him the wisdom[3] of the dragons, and sometimes she would simply stand guard[4] whilst he dreamt. As a child, he believed that the dragon was real, made of

1 **casually** – *wie unabsichtlich, beiläufig, zufällig*
2 **to play a joke on sb.** – *einen Scherz mit jdm. treiben*
3 **wisdom** – *Weisheit*
4 **to stand guard** – *wachen*

flesh and blood and shimmering[1] armoured scales[2] and simply invisible to adults for some reason or other.

Later, he realised that the facts of the matter were probably somewhat different. Sarantuya does exist, in a way, but she exists with her dragon-kindred[3] in another world. This world is as real and tangible[4] as the world of his clan, of his family, but far, far away. Further away than the mountains behind the horizon. Recently, Sarantuya's visits have become less frequent. She does not come every night now, but only now and then, usually when there are important things to discuss or a crucial[5] decision to be made. Sometimes, he is not aware of how important a decision is until she appears to him. Yet since they fled, since his life has gone so badly wrong, she has only come every now and then. It seems to have something to do with him growing up, and he notices this when he is near Arbesa. Just looking at her can fill him with feelings that are confusing, sometimes scary.

Is Sarantuya the dragon... jealous[6]? She has been the most important thing in his life up until now. He could cry to her[7] when he had hurt himself, she comforted[8] him with soothing[9] words when someone had done him wrong, and offered him advice when he did not know what to do.

Yet the first time he really followed her advice against his own personal convictions[10] it cost many of his tribe their lives. His future, which before seemed so sure, has become a hurricane[11], filled every day with new horrors and new uncertainties[12].

"There's somebody there."

1 **to shimmer** – *schimmern*
2 **armoured scales** – *Panzerschuppen*
3 **kindred (altertümlich)** – *Familie, Seinesgleichen*
4 **tangible** – *greifbar*
5 **crucial** – *sehr wichtig*
6 **jealous** – *eifersüchtig*
7 **to cry to sb.** – *sich bei jdm. ausweinen*
8 **to comfort** – *trösten*
9 **soothing** – *beruhigend, tröstend*
10 **conviction** – *Überzeugung*
11 **hurricane** – *Wirbelsturm*
12 **uncertainty** – *Unsicherheit*

It takes a moment for him to realise that this is Arbesa's voice, not the dragon's. She is sitting upright, the blanket has fallen from her shoulders and he can feel the cold. Her eyes are wide, full of fear.

Now he too can hear the noise. It is wrong that Arbesa heard it before him. He is the only warrior left in his clan, and he should be the one to keep watch over his betrothed[1]. It should not be his wife-to-be who watches over him.

Without making a sound, he sits up and reaches for his sword. He has already drawn it from its scabbard[2] and laid its bare blade[3] next to him to make sure that he will not have to make any more noise if an enemy approaches. With his free hand, he gestures[4] to Arbesa to watch his mother.

The sword belonged to his father and is longer than Timucin's arm. Actually, it is too heavy for him. He takes it with both hands and moves in the direction of the noise, crouching[5] as he goes. He can't hear anything now, though, but he thinks he can feel that he is not alone.

A moment later, he knows for sure that he is not alone. Cold, sharp steel is at his throat, not cutting him, but letting him feel its burn.

"If I were a Merkit or a Tajin, you would already be dead by now, my little Khan, and I would take your horses and your women," says a voice whispering in his ear. The whispering gives way to a raw laugh, the blade disappears from his neck, and he gets a rough shove[6] between his shoulder blades and stumbles[7] forward. It is difficult for him to keep his balance[8], but he does and then turns round, growls[9] angrily and lifts his sword. Behind him, a gigantic form comes out of the shadow into the moonlight, the laughing starts again and now sounds so scornful that Ti-

1 **betrothed (altertümlich)** – *Verlobte(r)*
2 **to draw a sword from a scabbard** – *ein Schwert aus der Scheide ziehen*
3 **bare blade** – *blanke Klinge*
4 **to gesture to sb. to do sth.** – *jdm. mit der Hand bedeuten, etw. zu tun*
5 **to crouch** – *sich ducken*
6 **shove** – *Stoß*
7 **to stumble** – *stolpern*
8 **to keep one's balance** – *das Gleichgewicht nicht verlieren*
9 **to growl** – *knurren*

mucin feels a flash of white rage[1] and is about to turn around and lunge at[2] the black monster behind him.

Instead, struggling to control himself[3], he asks: "Who are you?

"I'm someone who has just given you life, my little Khan," answers the voice, which he suddenly recognises from somewhere.

"On the other hand, it would barely have been worth[4] getting my sword dirty. Those two donkeys are worthless and, looking at your women, one is too old and the other is too young!"

Then his lowers his sword and steps closer to Timucin. Timucin's fear turns to confusion and disbelief[5]. The giant shrinks[6] back to normal size, then down to the size of a young man. Timucin's eyes widen.

"Chuzir?" he mumbles[7].

"Well, at least my Khan still knows the name of one of his best warriors," says Chuzir, "what an honour!"

"Chuzir?" asks Timucin again. Then he shouts the name as loud as he can, throws his sword down and wraps Chuzir in his arms. For several minutes, they do nothing except hug, pat each other's shoulders and jab[8] each other in the ribs playfully. They laugh until Timucin is dizzy and the two of them are wheezing[9] from the effort. Eventually, they let go of one another and Timucin, in an almost celebratory[10] tone, shouts "Chuzir! My brother in oath[11]! How long has it been?!"

"At least a year, even if it feels like ten," answers Chuzir, laughing. His eyes are shimmering, and as Timucin notices this, he feels tears of joy[12] streaming down his cheeks.

1 **rage** – *Wut*
2 **to lunge at sb.** – *sich auf jdn. stürzen*
3 **struggling to control oneself** – *mühsam beherrscht*
4 **it would barely have been worth…** – *es hätte sich kaum gelohnt…*
5 **disbelief** – *Unglauben*
6 **to shrink** – *schrumpfen*
7 **to mumble** – *murmeln*
8 **to jab sb.** – *jdn. boxen, jdm. einen (leichten) Stoß verpassen*
9 **to wheeze** – *keuchen*
10 **celebratory** – *feierlich*
11 **brother in oath** – *Schwurbruder*
12 **joy** – *Freude*

Timucin is embarrassed, and tries to wipe[1] the tears out of his eyes without Chuzir noticing. He looks at him closely, and it really does look as if Chuzir is now more than a year older. He has grown, at least half a hand, perhaps even more. His shoulders are broader, and Timucin cannot say whether the shadow on his cheeks is just a shadow, or perhaps the first fluffy[2] signs of a beard. His voice is deeper than Timucin remembers, too, and there could be no doubt that his brother in oath was approaching manhood[3], was perhaps already a man.

Chuzir, too, uses the opportunity to size up[4] Timucin, but Timucin can't work out what Chuzir makes of[5] him. Chuzir's eyes flashed briefly with scorn, but after a seemingly endless moment, he bows[6] his head and then drops to one knee.

"My Khan," he says.

"Well, that's better than 'my little Khan', I suppose," says a jeering[7] voice behind them. Timucin turns round, scared, and Chuzir too stands up, tense[8] and ready to fight. It only takes a moment, however, for his face to lighten[9] again. Then he speaks, and his voice is at once respectful and yet clearly amused.

"Arbesa! Look at you! You've become a woman!" he says, and then in an aside[10] to Timucin, "and a bit of a wild one, too, it would appear." He winks[11], "but I must apologise, for she will make a wonderful wife and defend her khan with all her might[12]."

1 **to wipe** – *wischen*
2 **fluffy** – *flaumig*
3 **manhood** – *Mannesalter*
4 **to size sb. up** – *jdn. kritisch mustern*
5 **to make sth. of sb.** – *jdn. einschätzen*
6 **to bow** – *senken*
7 **jeering** – *spöttisch*
8 **tense** – *angespannt*
9 **to lighten** – *aufhellen*
10 **aside** – *Bemerkung*
11 **to wink** – *zwinkern*
12 **might** – *Kraft*

It takes a second for Timucin to realise what he means: Arbesa is still looking at Chuzir with an expression of undisguised mistrust[1], holding a short dagger with a bent blade in her hand.

"Put the knife down, Arbesa," he says, laughing, "it's Chuzir, my brother in oath. Don't you recognise him?"

Arbesa hesitates[2] for a moment longer than Timucin thinks appropriate[3] and then nods without putting away her weapon. She keeps looking at the boy sceptically, and Timucin is confused and slightly hurt. Chuzir was not just his friend, but his brother in oath. This means that everything said against Chuzir was said against Timucin himself.

He gets a grip of his thoughts and says to himself that Arbesa does not know Chuzir very well, and while she has been a part of Timucin's life for a long time now, Chuzir does not know Arbesa very well either. Less than one month after he had returned from living in the village of his bride, Chuzir and his family had left the camp. Chuzir and Arbesa had not seen each other since then. Nevertheless, Timucin would have liked his future wife to show a little more respect for his brother in oath.

It is as if she has read his thoughts, and now wants to show him what she thinks: "Why did you creep up on us[4]? Are you alone?" she asks curtly[5].

"I didn't creep up," says Chuzir, which is a complete lie, "and I'm alone – for which you may be thankful[6], my lady."

The furrow in Arbesa's brow deepens[7] and her face takes on an expression of fury.

DRACHENFRAGE

Why is an insult made to Chuzir also an insult to Timucin?

1 **undisguised mistrust** – *unverhohlenes Misstrauen*
2 **to hesitate** – *zögern*
3 **appropriate** – *angemessen*
4 **to creep up on sb.** – *sich an jdn. heranschleichen*
5 **curt** – *schroff, spröde*
6 **for which you may be thankful** – *zu deinem Glück*
7 **to deepen** – *vertiefen*

Chuzir laughs, turns to Timucin and slaps him so heavily on the shoulder that his knee buckles slightly[1].

"She's alright[2], you know," he says, "just take good care of her: you won't find another like her so soon."

Not that he intends to[3] find another, but Timucin doesn't reply because he has the feeling that no matter what he says, Arbesa will use it against him. He picks up his sword and gestures to Chuzir to follow him.

"I can't offer you much, brother, but I do have space at my fire and a little cold meat."

"That is more than I have had for three days," answers Chuzir, but does not move to follow him. Instead, he picks up his sword and goes in the opposite[4] direction.

"Perhaps you can relight the fire to which you have invited me," he says with a scornful tone in his voice again. "In the meantime, I'll go and get my horse." Then he walks off before Timucin can say another word.

1 **his knee buckles slightly** – *er geht ein Stück weit in die Knie*
2 **alright** – *schon recht*
3 **to intend to do sth.** – *etw. vorhaben*
4 **opposite** – *entgegengesetzt*

Friend or Foe?

TR. 03

For a while, Timucin just stays standing where he is, looking at the direction in which Chuzir has left. Then he turns to Arbesa and gestures at the knife. She is still holding it so tight that all the blood has drained out of her fingers[1].

"Put it away, will you?" The words are supposed to sound[2] like a reproach[3], but he just can't get enough anger into his voice. Instead, he feels very warm and deeply touched[4].

Chuzir is right: after his dream-dragon, Arbesa is the best thing that has ever happened to him in his life[5]. She couldn't have known that it was Chuzir. She could only see an armed, dark form, and she had not hesitated to jump to his defence. Could he ask any more of the woman to whom he was betrothed?

Back at the camp, Arbesa crouches down to the remains of the fire and blows at the embers[6]. Within moments, a little yellow flame is licking at the air, and she skilfully[7] turns this into a new fire. She lays the knife down next to her, but does not put it away, and after a while she speaks:

"He knew that our fire was dead."

"Because he would have seen the glow if it had been lit," answers Timucin. "He has sharp eyes."

"He was listening to us," she insists. "Don't you find it odd[8], him turning up here at just this moment[9]?"

Timucin thinks hard about what a halfway plausible answer might sound like. Behind him, Chuzir speaks:

1 **all the blood has drained out of her fingers** – *alles Blut ist aus ihren Fingern gewichen*
2 **supposed to sound like…** – *sollten klingen wie…*
3 **reproach** – *Zurechtweisung, Vorwurf*
4 **touched** – *gerührt, bewegt*
5 **the best thing that's ever happened to sb.** – *das Beste, was jdm. jemals widerfahren ist*
6 **embers** – *Glut*
7 **skilfully** – *geschickt*
8 **odd** – *komisch*
9 **at just this moment** – *ausgerechnet jetzt*

"I would have overtaken you more quickly if you hadn't been so fast and if you hadn't covered up your tracks so well. You really do not make it easy to hunt[1] you."

"Is that what you're doing then," asks Arbesa coolly, "hunting us?"

Chuzir ties the harness of his horse to a bush. The horse looks healthy and its harness is magnificent[2].

"Hunting? Well that depends whether you are the prey[3]…"

Timucin doesn't like this answer, but he doesn't let the ugly thoughts that follow from it take hold. He kneels down to the fire, and Chuzir looks at Arbesa with an expression that he likes even less. Then his brother in oath asks him:

"Is your mother ill?"

Timucin looks over to Üdschin and notices that she is awake, but clearly prefers to pretend to be asleep.

"She's got a fever, but she is strong."

Arbesa goes to fetch[4] the meat while Chuzir also opens the bag on his horse's saddle[5] and pulls out a very welcome present: two water-bags, filled with clear water: they drink as much of this as Chuzir eats of their meat.

After a while, Üdschin stops pretending to sleep and takes her share of this improvised[6] feast[7]. She does not eat much, but drinks long, deep draughts[8] of Chuzir's water. After she had emptied the first bag, she gives it back to Chuzir with a look of embarrassment and declines his offer of the second bag.

---

1 **to hunt** - *jagen*
2 **magnificent** - *prachtvoll*
3 **prey** - *Beute*
4 **to fetch** - *holen*
5 **saddle** - *Sattel*
6 **improvised** - *improvisiert*
7 **feast** - *Festmahl, Gelage*
8 **draught** - *Zug*

"Go ahead, drink as much as you want, my lady," says Chuzir, "for there is a stream not more than half an hour's ride[1] from here that is not frozen over yet."

"We must have missed it," answers Üdschin. Her voice is not at all reproachful[2], but Timucin is embarrassed nevertheless. Chuzir gives Üdschin the bag and then goes to his horse, returning with a small pouch[3]. As he opens it, Timucin smells aykol, a strong potion[4] made from mare's milk[5] that the men in his father's yurt used to drink so much of. He turns it down[6] as Chuzir holds it out to him. Chuzir shrugs his shoulders[7] and then takes a mouthful[8]. Timucin has never had aykol: he hates the taste, and he often saw how aggressive and uninhibited[9] the men became when they had drunk too much of it.

"Perhaps next year," says Chuzir. Timucin understands what he is trying to say, but does not react. He is used to Chuzir's little jabs[10], though. They have been part of their friendship for as long as he can remember.

Arbesa, however, snatches the pouch from Chuzir's hand[11] and takes a mouthful that is clearly deeper than the one he has just taken. Without flinching[12], she hands it back to him, and Chuzir looks impressed. He turns back to Timucin.

"I can't tell you how happy I am to see you again – alive. I had almost given up hope. I was so angry with myself[13]."

1 **half an hour's ride** – *ein halbstündiger Ritt*
2 **not at all reproachful** – *frei von jedem Vorwurf*
3 **pouch** – *Beutel*
4 **potion** – *Trunk, Gebräu*
5 **mare's milk** – *Stutenmilch*
6 **to turn down sth.** – *ablehnen*
7 **to shrug one's shoulders** – *mit den Achseln zucken*
8 **mouthful** – *(kräftiger) Schluck*
9 **uninhibited** – *unbeherrscht, hemmungslos*
10 **jab** – *Stichelei*
11 **to snatch sth. from sb.'s hand** – *jdm. etw. aus der Hand reißen*
12 **without flinching** – *ohne mit der Wimper zu zucken; ohne die Miene zu verziehen*
13 **I was so angry with myself** – *ich habe mir solche Vorwürfe gemacht*

"And not without cause[1]!" says Arbesa. Üdschin looks at her angrily and Timucin shouts at her: "Silence! What nonsense is this?[2]"

"She is right," says Chuzir sadly, "for if my father and I had not gone away..."

"... exactly the same thing would have happened!" interrupts[3] Üdschin. Her voice is shaky[4], but still has the authority it used to have when she was the wife of the khan. "If you had all stayed, your father, your brother and you, it would not have changed anything."

"But we would never have..." Chuzir begins. Timucin's mother interrupts him again.

"Your father would never have fought against[5] the rebellion, your brother neither," she says, shaking her head sadly and taking another mouthful of water, "and even if they had, they would probably now be just as dead as the very few who remained loyal[6] to the rightful[7] khan. She nods to Chuzir: "So do not be angry at yourself, my lad[8]. Your father was right to do as he did."

"My father would never have broken his oath," says Chuzir, "for he was a man of his word[9]!"

"Was?" asks Timucin, alarmed.

For a second, Chuzir's face falls[10], but he bites his bottom lip and does not answer Timucin's question.

1 **not without cause** – *nicht zu Unrecht*
2 **What nonsense is this?** – *Was redest du für einen Unsinn?*
3 **to interrupt** – *jdm. ins Wort fallen, unterbrechen*
4 **shaky** – *zitternd*
5 **to fight against sth.** – *sich gegen etw. stellen*
6 **to remain loyal to sb.** – *jdm. die Treue halten*
7 **rightful** – *rechtmäßig*
8 **lad** – *Junge*
9 **man of his word** – *Ehrenmann*
10 **his face falls** – *er verliert die Kontrolle über seine Züge*

"I did not want to leave, but my father drove the flock[1] onto an open pasture[2]."

"And you and your brother simply obeyed[3] your father," says Üdschin, "so there is nothing for you to be ashamed of[4]."

Timucin nods his agreement to what his mother has said, but Arbesa frowns[5] in a very expressive manner. Yet she does not say anything, which Timucin is silently grateful for. He too has to keep control of his feelings[6], and this is not the first time that he catches himself wondering[7] if it really was chance that Chuzir's father left with his family to look for fresh pastures just two days before that fateful morning. Chuzir still looks angry, so Timucin speaks:

"If anyone is at fault[8], then it is me."

"Rubbish!" shouts Chuzir, but Timucin just shakes his head and continues: "It was my decision not to attack the Tatars and to pay the ransom[9]. If I had just listened to the warriors of the tribe..."

"Then we would all be dead, and there would be no Kijat clan whatsoever," interrupts his mother, softly but firmly. There is a slight reproach in these words, but Timucin chooses not to hear at this point.

"The Tatars have hundreds more warriors than we did. What chance would we have stood[10]?"

"What do chances matter when it is a matter of honour?" asks Chuzir.

1 **flock** – *Herde*
2 **pasture** – *Weide*
3 **to obey sb.** – *jdm. gehorchen*
4 **there is nothing for you to be ashamed of** – *es gibt nichts, was du dir vorzuwerfen hättest*
5 **to frown** – *die Stirn runzeln*
6 **to keep control of one's feelings** – *seine Gefühle mäßigen*
7 **to catch oneself wondering if...** – *sich beim Gedanken ertappen, ob...*
8 **to be at fault** – *schuld sein*
9 **ransom** – *Lösegeld*
10 **to stand a chance** – *eine Chance haben*

Both Arbesa and Üdschin sigh[1] deeply. They say nothing, but Timucin sees them roll their eyes[2] – and sees that this does not escape Chuzir's notice[3] either.

"Tell me what happened," says Chuzir after an uncomfortable silence[4].

"The men listened to me in the end," answers Timucin, "well, perhaps not to me, but to the son of the khan at least. So instead of reaching for our swords and trying to free my father as Ilhan's father – and many others – suggested, we paid the ransom and hoped the Tatars would keep their end of the bargain[5]." Chuzir laughs roughly at this.

"Tatars? Keep up their end of a bargain?!" he repeats in a derogatory[6] tone. It sounds as if he wishes to curse[7] and has replaced the word with "Tatars".

"They did keep up their end of the bargain," says Arbesa bitterly, "and sent him back three days later."

"Poisoned[8], and more dead than alive," adds Timucin, even more bitterly. "He stayed alive for two days and then died in agony[9]. Then they attacked us."

Chuzir looks sadly at him, but is not at all surprised. Timucin is sure that he has already heard the story, but he continues. He feels the need to tell it[10]; perhaps it would help him in his grief[11]."

1 **to sigh** – *seufzen*
2 **to roll one's eyes** – *die Augen verdrehen*
3 **to escape sb.'s notice** – *jdm. entgehen*
4 **uncomfortable silence** – *unbehagliches Schweigen*
5 **to keep one's end of the bargain** – *ehrenhaft sein, seine Versprechen einhalten*
6 **derogatory** – *abfällig*
7 **to curse** – *fluchen*
8 **poisoned** – *vergiftet*
9 **to die in agony** – *elendig sterben, unter Qualen sterben*
10 **he feels the need to tell it** – *es ist ihm ein Bedürfnis, es zu erzählen*
11 **grief** – *Trauer*

"Many of the warriors called for revenge[1] and wanted to move against[2] the Tatars," he says, "except Tedschen and his son Ilhan. Tedschen declared himself the new khan[3], and most of the men sided with him[4].

"But you were the new khan," says Chuzir angrily, "and you still are!"

"Well, Tedschen and many of the other men did not see it that way," says Üdschin bitterly. "Think of it: a young, inexperienced[5] lad, not to mention the bastard child of the khan and a Merkit he brought into the tribe twenty years ago." She shakes her head and stares into the fire for a moment: "It wasn't hard for Tedschen to convince the others that he was the rightful khan of the Kijat. They chased us out: me, my son and his betrothed."

"But why didn't you go to the Voshon?" says Chuzir, confused. "Arbesa's father would surely have offered you shelter[6]!"

"We wanted to," says Arbesa, "but on the second day of our journey, the Tajin warriors appeared[7]. They took or destroyed[8] everything we had left. We had to flee with little more than what we had on our backs[9]".

"I would not be surprised if Tedschen had set them on our trail," says Timucin angrily. "He always was a coward[10] who left the dirty work to others[11] – just like his son." Timucin and Ilhan, Tedschen's son, have been enemies since their childhood.

"Perhaps they left him no choice," says Üdschin. Timucin looks at his mother a little disbelievingly[12]. Why is she trying to protect a man who has done them so much wrong? She continues: "The Merkits and the

1 **revenge** – *Rache*
2 **to move against sb.** – *gegen jdn. ziehen*
3 **to declare oneself sth.** – *sich selbst zu etw. ausrufen*
4 **to side with sb.** – *sich auf jds. Seite stellen*
5 **inexperienced** – *unerfahren*
6 **shelter** – *Unterschlupf*
7 **to appear** – *auftauchen*
8 **to destroy** – *zerstören*
9 **little more than what we had on our backs** – *wenig mehr als dem, was wir auf dem Leib hatten*
10 **coward** – *Feigling*
11 **to leave the dirty work to others** – *anderen das schmutzige Tun überlassen*
12 **disbelievingly** – *ungläubig*

Tajin have always been allies[1]. They probably forced Tedschen to get rid of us[2]."

Chuzir, too, eyes[3] Üdschin sceptically and then turns back to Timucin. "So you've been on the run[4] since then? That's almost a year!"

"We were hoping that they would lose our trail or get tired of hunting us," says Arbesa.

"But they haven't," adds Timucin, "and I have failed as khan."

Chuzir gives him an odd look – Timucin cannot decide how it is meant[5] – and then takes another sip of aykol, before shaking his head vigorously.

"The Tajin are known to be cowards without any form of honour[6]," he says, "but they are also known as good trackers[7] and even better hunters. If you had failed, you would not have survived a full year."

"What about five? Five years?" says Timucin darkly. "I know that they will not give up."

Chuzir does not contradict[8] him, but simply looks at him thoughtfully[9] for a moment before asking another question.

"So where are you headed to[10] now?"

Timucin takes so long to answer that what he says is robbed of any credibility it may have had[11].

DRACHENFRAGE

Why, in Üdschin's opinion, was it so easy for Tedschen to turn the Kijats against Timucin?

1 **ally** – *Verbündeter*
2 **to get rid of sb.** – *jdn. fortjagen, loswerden*
3 **to eye sb.** – *jdn. beäugen, jdn. anschauen*
4 **on the run** – *auf der Flucht*
5 **to decide how sth. is meant** – *etw. deuten*
6 **honour** – *Ehre*
7 **tracker** – *Spurenleser*
8 **to contradict sb.** – *jdm. widersprechen*
9 **thoughtfully** – *nachdenklich*
10 **Where are you headed to?** – *Wohin seid ihr jetzt unterwegs?*
11 **robbed of any credibility it may have had** – *jeder Glaubwürdigkeit beraubt, die sie jemals vielleicht besaß*

"We make for[1] Burchan Chaldun."

"The Holy Mountain? So you mean to ask Tenghis for counsel[2]?" asks Chuzir, a distinctly scornful tone in his voice. Timucin does not answer.

"And what will you do then?" continues Chuzir.

"Then?" replies Timucin.

Chuzir makes a reluctant[3] gesture, takes a third, deeper swig[4] of aykol and then passes the pouch to Arbesa. She shakes her head and glowers at him[5] with fire in her eyes.

"Well, what will you do if Tenghis does not send thunder and lightning from the heavens to burn the Tajin?" asks Chuzir. Timucin shrugs his shoulders[6] helplessly.

"Perhaps we'll just keep going. The lands north of Burchan Chaldun are unknown; nobody can say who lives there."

"Nobody can say whether they actually exist," answers Chuzir pointedly[7]. "Some even claim[8] that the world ends after the Holy Mountain!"

"What nonsense," snorts[9] Arbesa, "as if the world could just stop somewhere!"

"Others claim that there is nothing but wild tribes there who kill everyone who dares[10] to set so much as a foot on their land!" continues Chuzir unchecked[11]. "In any case, no one has ever returned from those parts. Perhaps there is a monster there!"

Perhaps there are dragons.

"Or perhaps it's just so nice there that no one ever wants to come back," says Arbesa.

1 **to make for sth. (altertümlich)** – *sich auf den Weg machen nach*
2 **counsel** – *Rat*
3 **reluctant** – *unwillig*
4 **swig** – *Schluck*
5 **to glower at sb.** – *jdn. finster ansehen*
6 **to shrug one's shoulders** – *mit den Achseln zucken*
7 **pointedly** – *betont*
8 **to claim that** – *etw. behaupten*
9 **to snort** – *schnauben*
10 **to dare to do sth.** – *es wagen, etw. zu tun*
11 **unchecked** – *unbeirrt, unbeeindruckt*

"Be that as it may[1]," answers Chuzir, "you can't stay here whatever you do. The Tajin are on your heels[2], and although I laid a few false tracks, that won't keep them off for long. We need to move."

"We?" asks Timucin. Chuzir laughs.

"I've been looking for you for almost a year, brother," he says, "and now I find you in direst need[3]. Do you really think that I would just leave you alone without us having at least got drunk together?" With that, he holds the pouch out to Timucin.

1 **be that as it may** – *sei's drum*
2 **to be on sb.'s heels** – *jdm. auf den Fersen sein*
3 **direst need** – *höchste Not*

The Holy Mountain

TR. 04

They do not reach the Holy Mountain the day after. Or the day after that. Only on the evening of the third day do they arrive in time to set up camp[1] under the trees. The desert has given way to a marshy[2] steppe, and the steppe has then become a hilly scrubland[3]. This, in turn, has become a wintry[4] woodland of bare[5] trees. Whilst these leafless[6] trees offer some protection from the icy wind and the worst of the cold[7], it is going to become even more difficult to cover their tracks[8] if the Tajin are still following them. And Timucin does not doubt for one moment that they are following him. They've been hunting them for almost a year. Why should they give up now, now that there is almost nowhere left to where they can flee?

He sleeps badly that night. Once again, Sarantuya does not come to him, and he awakes under the grey skies of approaching dawn before the others. He will cover the last part of the journey alone. Üdschin's fever has lessened[9], but she is still too weak to join him as he climbs the mountain. Arbesa too is weak, although she is brave and tries to not to show it. Nonetheless, she cannot hide the fact that[10] she is nearing the end of her strength. It is hardly surprising given that they have been fleeing for almost a year now with no respite[11].

Of course, Chuzir has offered to come with him on this last stage, and Timucin would like nothing better than to take him because, if he is honest, he is afraid of setting foot on the forbidden mountain. Yet he

1 **to set up camp** – *ein Lager aufschlagen*
2 **marshy** – *morastig*
3 **scrubland** – *Buschland*
4 **wintry** – *winterlich*
5 **bare** – *kahl*
6 **leafless** – *blattlos*
7 **the worst of the cold** – *die ärgste Kälte*
8 **to cover one's tracks** – *die Spuren verwischen*
9 **to lessen** – *zurückgehen*
10 **she cannot hide the fact that…** – *sie kann nicht mehr verhehlen, dass…*
11 **with no respite** – *ununterbrochen, ohne Pause*

turns down the offer, asking him instead to stay at the camp and watch over Arbesa and his mother. Chuzir promises this in an almost ceremonial[1] fashion[2].Timucin sets off.

He leaves his sword, shield and armour[3] behind, taking nothing but his bow and one single arrow with him. The arrow is the precious[4] gift of friendship Chuzir has given to him. He has not been separated from it for more than an hour at a time since then.

In the clear light of the morning, the evenly-formed[5] ridge[6] of Burchan Chaldun seems almost near enough to reach out and touch, but he knows that he has quite some way to go. He walks quickly and soon realises that it is as bad as he has feared: the mountain is far steeper than it looks[7], and the woods appear to become thicker and more impenetrable[8] with every step he takes. It is as if nature is trying to stop him getting any further.

He tries to banish[9] this foolish thought and concentrates on nothing more than putting one foot in front of another. It gets more and more difficult to make a path, and now he starts to realise why they had the impression that the mountain was moving away every time they got closer to it: because the mountain is huge, and even its seemingly rounded top is far steeper than it looks.

The closer he gets to the peak[10], the steeper the slope he has to climb. During the final ascent[11], he is forced to use his bow as a walking stick[12] before climbing the last part. This is why they call it the forbidden moun-

1 **ceremonial** - *feierlich*
2 **fashion** - *Art, Weise*
3 **armour** - *Rüstung*
4 **precious** - *kostbar*
5 **evenly formed** - *gleichmäßig geformt*
6 **ridge** - *Bergzug, Buckel*
7 **steeper than it looks** - *steiler, als es den Anschein hat*
8 **impenetrable** - *undurchdringlich*
9 **to banish a thought** - *einen Gedanken verscheuchen*
10 **peak** - *Gifpel*
11 **ascent** - *Anstieg, Auffahrt*
12 **walking stick** - *Wanderstab*

tain, he realises: it might not be forbidden as such, but it is so difficult to climb that it might just as well be[1].

It is almost midday as he reaches his goal. He is exhausted[2], and he is not even sure whether it has been worthwhile[3].

Before he reaches the gods, he stops to sit and gather his strength. Arbesa would enjoy the view, he thinks, tired. If things had been different and they had not had to spend the last year just trying to survive, she would have been able to climb just for the view. As he looks out over the other side of the mountain, a fantastic panorama opens out before him and gives him a breathtaking[4] feeling of space. Or maybe he is just delirious[5] because of the thin air.

Timucin smiles at his own thoughts, slowly gets back up (which takes more effort than he likes to admit to himself) and walks the last few steps to the holy place. Until now, he has avoided looking at it. Perhaps because he is afraid of being burnt in flame for looking at Tenghis, as some claim, or perhaps because he is afraid of being disappointed.

At first, it looks more likely to be the latter[6]. Timucin does not really know what he had expected. Nothing particular, perhaps an impressive building or a temple, perhaps... well, anything. Some kind of sign that men have been here before, the graves of people sacrificed[7], a stone circle or rock drawings. Yet the top of the mountain looks untouched[8], as if he really is the first ever person to have come up.

Perhaps he is.

1 **it might just as well be (Redewendung)** – *es läuft auf dasselbe hinaus*
2 **exhausted** – *erschöpft*
3 **worthwhile** – *der Mühe wert*
4 **breathtaking** – *atemberaubend*
5 **delirious** – *phantasierend*
6 **the latter** – *Letzteres*
7 **sacrificed** – *geopfert*
8 **untouched** – *unberührt*

A sudden gust of wind[1] sweeps[2] over the summit[3]. His teeth chatter with cold. He remembers that he does not have much time, having promised Arbesa and his mother that he will return before sundown. And the climb down will doubtless be even more difficult than the ascent.

The top of the mountain is covered in grass that is starting to go yellow. It is smaller than the space taken up by his old village, and his village back then was a collection of little more than a dozen yurts. At its centre there is a heap of rocks[4] which, from a distance, might well look like a temple. Up here, it looks as if a young giant has thrown them one on top of another in some kind of game. Two rocks have been laid one over the other and form a kind of stone tent, or perhaps an entrance into the world of the gods in which Tenghis lives.

Timucin goes over, but then he remembers that it is not fitting[5] to go before a god with a weapon, so he leans the belt and his quiver with its precious arrow against the cliff. Then he enters the triangular gap[6] under the rocks.

It is, however, not a portal into the world of the gods, but simply a triangular opening that, after a few steps, ends in a wall of rock. Here, however, he sees the first signs of human life. There is a flat stone lying against the wall, and it has been too carefully placed to be there by chance. Furthermore, it is a different type of stone entirely, and he can see that it has been polished[7] smooth by countless[8] pairs of knees, perhaps over many centuries.

He goes to the stone, kneels on it and waits for something to happen, for him to feel the gods, the sublime[9], something. Yet nothing happens.

1 **gust of wind** – *Windstoß*
2 **to sweep** – *fegen*
3 **summit** – *Gipfel, Bergkuppe*
4 **heap of rocks** – *Haufen von Felsen*
5 **it is not fitting** – *es ziemt sich nicht*
6 **gap** – *Spalt*
7 **to polish** – *polieren*
8 **countless** – *zahllos*
9 **the sublime** – *das Erhabene*

Nothing. Except the fact that the cold is slowly creeping[1] into him because he has stopped moving.

Of course it was never going to be this easy, he thinks, annoyed at his own foolishness. All those long months they have spent on the road, he has prayed and pleaded with the gods for help[2], for enlightenment[3], or at least for advice. But they have remained silent. Why should they appear now, just because he has come?

Perhaps there is a certain prayer he needs to utter[4], a certain dance he needs to perform, or a certain sacrifice he needs to offer. He doesn't know. He is no shaman[5], and he was never particularly interested in them and their complicated ceremonies either. He regrets this now; perhaps the gods are far pettier[6] than he thought.

"Tenghis," he whispers, "I come to you to beg for help. Not for myself, because I know that I have earned no help. I have not prayed to you enough, and I have almost never been serious when I have prayed. When I have sacrificed, I have only sacrificed things it did not hurt me to give. So I have no right[7] to ask you for anything. Yet I ask you now to help Arbesa, and my mother. Üdschin is a pious[8] woman who has never acted against your commandments[9], neither has Arbesa. Punish me, if you will[10], yet do not punish my mother nor my betrothed for something I am guilty of."

TR. 05

He isn't really expecting an answer, but he gets one, even if it is completely different to the one he was expecting. Behind him, a deep, rum-

1 **to creep** – *kriechen*
2 **to plead with sb. for sth.** – *jdn. um etw. anflehen*
3 **enlightenment** – *Erleuchtung*
4 **to utter sth. (altertümlich)** – *etw. sprechen*
5 **shaman** – *Schamane*
6 **petty** – *kleinlich*
7 **I have no right to...** – *es steht mir nicht zu,...*
8 **pious** – *fromm*
9 **commandment** – *Gebot*
10 **if you will (altertümlich)** – *wenn du willst*

bling[1] laugh sounds out[2], and as he turns around, he just about sees a fleeting[3] flash[4] of gold as it disappears behind the rocks he is under.

Timucin comes out of the gap and looks around. He is as alone as he was before. He picks up his bow and quiver and walks around the pile of rocks to look out at the unknown lands on the other side of Burchan Chaldun. Grey fog covers the tops of the mountains and has sunk into the valleys between them like grey sheep's wool. Nevertheless, he can still feel the expansiveness[5] of the hilly country hidden before him, can still feel the huge flatness of the plains[6] behind it. He hears something behind him again, like the scrabbling[7] of gigantic claws over rocks. Now he sees that Sarantuya is there, a huge form in gold that darkens[8] the sun and looks down on him from an astonishing[9] height.

"Are you Tenghis?" he hears himself asking.

The answer is once again roaring laughter which seems to make the earth tremble[10], and a shake of the head. Sarantuya's golden scales[11] are jingling[12] and clinking[13] like the biggest cymbal[14] in the world.

"I think you know the answer to that, my little Khan," says the golden dragon.

Timucin looks up, his mouth open wide. It is the first time that he has really heard the full power of Sarantuya's voice. Until then, it has always been a silent whisper in his thoughts. It is also the first time he

1 **rumbling** - *grollend*
2 **to sound out** - *erschallen*
3 **fleeting** - *flüchtig*
4 **flash** - *Blitzen*
5 **expansiveness** - *Weite*
6 **the huge flatness of the plains** - *die weiten, flachen Ebenen*
7 **scrabbling** - *Scharren*
8 **to darken** - *verdunkeln*
9 **astonishing** - *unglaublich, atemberaubend, erstaunlich*
10 **to tremble** - *schütteln, beben*
11 **scale** - *Schuppe*
12 **to jingle** - *klimpern*
13 **to clink** - *klirren*
14 **cymbal** - *Zimbel*

has actually stood face-to-face with[1] the gigantic dragon. He has seen her countless times in his dreams, and she has often taken him into her dragon world, where he has stood next to her, touched her and even sat on her back to fly with her, higher than the highest cloud.

Now, however, he is really standing in front of her, and it takes him a few moments to realise what this really means: Sarantuya exists. She is not an imaginary friend[2], but a real being[3].

"But how do you know that you are not dreaming now, my little Khan?" asks Sarantuya, smiling.

"Because this is not a dream!" answers Timucin confidently[4].

"Why?"

Timucin is about to answer quite rudely, but then thinks better of it[5] and pulls down his gloves[6] far enough to pinch himself[7] so roughly on the wrist the tears well up[8] in his eyes.

"Aha," says Sarantuya, sounding a little bored, "and what is that supposed to prove[9]?" She runs her claws over the cliff[10], making an almost metallic sound, and leaves finger-deep scratches on the rock-face.

"It hurt, and that proves that I'm not dreaming," answers Timucin.

"Or it proves that you have just dreamt that you have hurt yourself," answers the dragon.

Timucin is still astonished[11] by Sarantuya's size in real life.

"Nonsense," he counters[12] angrily, "this is... I mean..."

1 **to stand face-to-face with sb.** – *jdm. gegenüberstehen*
2 **imaginary friend** – *ausgedachter Freund*
3 **being** – *Wesen*
4 **confidently** – *überzeugt, selbstbewusst*
5 **to think better of sth.** – *sich eines Besseren besinnen*
6 **glove** – *Handschuh*
7 **to pinch oneself** – *sich kneifen*
8 **to well up** – *aufkommen, aufwallen*
9 **What is that supposed to prove?** – *Was soll das beweisen?*
10 **cliff** – *Fels*
11 **to be astonished** – *staunen*
12 **to counter** – *widersprechen*

"Yes?" asks Sarantuya, leaning her head to the side. Timucin starts to feel where this thought is leading and stops. Instead, he asks Sarantuya a question in a deliberately[1] reproachful tone:

"You're not reading my thoughts, are you?"

"I am a part of you, so it can't be otherwise[2], can it, my little Khan?"

"Don't call me that," says Timucin annoyed, "I have a name!"

"Really?" Sarantuya blinks[3] and her gigantic, scaly tail twitches[4]. Timucin has the feeling that something else is moving behind it, something invisible[5] and much, much bigger. Suddenly, the dragon grins, which looks as odd as it does disturbing[6].

"Is this going to be our first real argument[7]?" She giggles[8] and it sounds as if chunks[9] of rock are rolling down an icy cliff: "But never mind. In that case, I'll call you Genghis from now on."

"That is not my name!" answers Timucin.

"Not yet!" replies the dragon. With every word she speaks, her scornful grin not only starts to fade[10], but becomes different, frightening, just like her voice.

"Yet you will be called it. People will know this name from one end of the world to the other, believe you me!"

"You once told me that you could not tell me anything about my future," says Timucin, worried. Genghis Khan[11]? The name has a strange sound, and not a particularly pleasant one, he thinks. Then again[12], it is

1 **deliberately** – *bewusst*
2 **it can't be otherwise** – *das bleibt nicht aus*
3 **to blink** – *blinzeln*
4 **to twitch** – *zucken*
5 **invisible** – *unsichtbares*
6 **disturbing** – *verstörend*
7 **argument** – *Streit, Auseinandersetzung*
8 **to giggle** – *kichern*
9 **chunk** – *Brocken*
10 **to fade** – *verblassen*
11 **Genghis Khan** – *Dschingis Khan (der bekannte Khan der Mongolen, er lebte ca. 1155–1227)*
12 **then again** – *andererseits*

exciting, in a completely new way. It seems to contain[1] a promise[2] of some kind, although he can't say what it is.

"What of it[3]?" asks Sarantuya, annoyed: "Do you never do anything that you shouldn't?" Timucin does not answer.

"I only tell you what is going to happen anyway," continues the dragon, "and whatever you do, you cannot change the fact that, one day, the whole world will know you by this name, little... er, *Genghis* Khan. Nevertheless, the most important decision is yours to make."

"And what decision is that?" asks Timucin. *Genghis Khan.* He repeats the name a few times in his mind, and something weird[4] happens: it frightens him.

"The most important question of all, my little Khan," answers Sarantuya, now quite serious, "which is whether you want people to speak your name with respect or with fear." Her dragon-face turns thoughtful. "Or perhaps both."

"You are pulling my leg[5]," answers Timucin, mainly with the aim of hiding the fear he feels listening to these words. For they have a truth he cannot deny[6].

"Now, I don't have all the time in the world, little Khan, and neither do you. So tell me why you came."

"What else have you got to do that is so important?" asks Timucin.

"Dragon's business," answers Sarantuya curtly[7]. "Now, what is it?"

"I don't know," admits[8] Timucin hesitantly, "I thought... I thought that..."

"That I would tell you?" says Sarantuya once he has finished talking and is moving from one foot to the other. "There is nothing I can tell you that you don't already know," she says, sighing deeply, "but I can tell

1 **to contain** – *beinhalten*
2 **promise** – *Versprechen*
3 **What of it? (altertümlich)** – *Na und?*
4 **weird** – *unheimlich*
5 **to pull sb.'s leg** – *jdm. auf den Arm nehmen*
6 **to deny a truth** – *die Wahrheit leugnen*
7 **curtly** – *schnippisch*
8 **to admit** – *gestehen*

you what you know and do not want to admit to yourself. Would you like that?"

Timucin nods.

"You are not here to pray to a god you do not believe in."

"That is not true!" says Timucin, frightened: "Tenghis is our god! He created the world and everything that lives in it, and he watches over us and protects us!"

"Well, he doesn't protect you so much, but..." quips[1] the dragon.

"That is not true either!" objects[2] Timucin: "It was Tedschen who betrayed[3] us! If it weren't for[4] him and the Tatars, none of this would have happened. We would still be in our camp and..." He is silent for a moment and then shrugs his shoulders helplessly.

Sarantuya does not bother answering, but looks at him for a while with an inscrutable[5] expression before moving slowly, majestically past him to the other end of the summit. She looks out at the foggy landscape on the other side of Burchan Chaldun.

"Is that why you are here, young Genghis?" she asks.

"Nonsense!" counters Timucin, but without real conviction[6] in his voice.

"You don't know it, but deep down[7], you are tired of all this running away," continues the dragon. "You have been fleeing for a year now, and have lost everything that you once had and everything you were attached to[8]. You don't want to run any more, but how can you fight? You are still too young and inexperienced."

"I am a Khan!" objects Timucin.

1 **to quip** – *spöttisch/witzelnd antworten,*
2 **to object** – *aufbegehren*
3 **to betray** – *verraten*
4 **if it weren't for** – *ohne*
5 **inscrutable** – *undeutbar*
6 **without real conviction** – *ohne Überzeugung*
7 **deep down** – *tief im Innersten*
8 **everything you were attached to** – *alles, woran eure Herzen gehangen haben*

"You are the khan of a tribe which consists of[1] you, your mother and your betrothed," answers the dragon, shaking her head.

"And Chuzir," he snorts.

Sarantuya turns her heavy head and looks at him silently for a while. He tries to decipher[2] a meaning from her scaly face, but he cannot.

"You must be patient, little Genghis," she says after some time, "but it will not take long for many things in your life to change, if not everything."

"How long?" asks Timucin, excited. "Another year? Another five? I can't wait any longer!"

"You humans!" sighs the dragon. "Your lives are so short, over almost as soon as they begin, and yet you simply cannot wait for the few years you do have to pass." She nods towards the grey sea of fog out of which a few mountain peaks, covered in scratches[3], are jutting out[4].

"You hope that you will find peace there, a place for you and your family to live out your days. Your future does not lie there, my little Genghis."

For a second, Timucin seriously considers asking the dragon to call him 'my little Khan' again. The name Genghis fills him with fear[5], but he also realises that it will make everything worse.

"Why? Because there are monsters there?" he asks.

"Oh yes, of course, the worst you can imagine!" says Sarantuya, laughing: "These monsters are called people! No, believe me, your place is not there. This land needs you."

Me? thinks Timucin, me? With nothing more than the clothes I have on my back. I who have[6] lost everything and after a year of running am now both at the end of my strength and quite literally[7] at the end of the world?

1 **to consist of sth.** – *aus etw. bestehen*
2 **to decipher** – *entziffern*
3 **covered in scratches** – *zerschunden*
4 **to jut out** – *aus etw. ragen*
5 **to fill somebody with fear** – *jdm. Furcht einflößen*
6 **I who...** – *ich, der ich...*
7 **literally** – *buchstäblich*

"Listen to me," continues Sarantuya, realising that he will not say what she wants him to, "I can't tell you what your future will bring, but perhaps I can help you find the right way."

"What, just like you did a year ago?"

Sarantuya looks at him quizzically[1], sadly. As she can read his thoughts – thoughts which are hers too in a way[2] – she knows exactly what he means. Nevertheless, for some reason or another[3] she wants him to say it out loud.

"After the Tatars had taken my father, the men of the tribe wanted to reach for their weapons and free him by force[4], as honour requires!"

"And you didn't want to do that?" asks Sarantuya.

"Yes, I did!" answers Timucin, himself a little surprised at his own honesty, "I did very much. But I did not do so, because I listened to you and took the way of the coward instead of that of the warrior, and I lost everything!"

"Sometimes, that is the way it is[5]," says the dragon softly, "it is never easy to go a new way, and sometimes it has to get worse before it can get better."

"What could be worse?" he snaps[6].

"A lot!" answers the dragon: "It can – and will – get worse. Soon. You are going to go through a lot of pain for a long time."

"Is that why you called me here," asks Timucin, "to make me afraid?"

"That's odd. I had the feeling that it was *you* who called *me*," smiles Sarantuya, before her face once again becomes serious. She stretches out one of her claws, which is big and strong enough to tear an ox[7] to pieces and yet soft and nimble[8] like the hands of a musician who can play the

1 **quizzically** – *fragend*
2 **in a way** – *irgendwie*
3 **for some reason or another** – *aus irgendeinem Grund*
4 **by force** – *mit Gewalt*
5 **that is the way it is (Redewendung)** – *so ist es*
6 **to snap** – *fauchen*
7 **ox** – *Ochse*
8 **nimble** – *geschickt, wendig*

most delicate[1] of tones on his instrument. She carefully removes the arrow of friendship from his quiver, examines[2] it for a moment and then puts it back just as gently[3] as she has removed it. Timucin wonders whether this has a meaning, but the dragon starts to speak again.

DRACHENFRAGE

Timucin meets Sarantuya again in this chapter. What is different about the way she looks and sounds?

"A time of pain is before you, little Genghis. You will betray the person you love the most and be betrayed by the person you trust[4] the most. You will have doubts, you will be desperate and you will believe that there is no way forward and that only death will relieve you of your pain[5]. Yet you must believe me when I say that all this is necessary for you to reach the right decision in the end."

"Just like last year?" he asks, bitterly, wishing to hurt Sarantuya. She sighs, very deeply and very sadly.

"It is probably too much to ask that you understand everything now," she says, "but think of what I have said to you. Now you must go. Both of us have urgent[6] tasks[7] to take care of."

"Dragon's business?" he asks.

"Khan's business," replies the dragon, "well, at least in your case. Now, make haste[8], little Genghis, for you do not have much time."

1 **delicate** – *zart*
2 **to examine** – *begutachten*
3 **gently** – *sanft*
4 **to trust sb.** – *jdm. vertrauen*
5 **to relieve sb. of sth.** – *jdn. von etw. erlösen*
6 **urgent** – *dringend*
7 **task** – *Aufgabe*
8 **to make haste (altertümlich)** – *sich sputen*

Betrayal[1]

TR. 06

It seems as if luck is on his side at least once today. Just as he feared, the descent[2] is far more difficult than the ascent, and his hopes of reaching Arbesa and his mother before dark start to fade. After about an hour or so, however, he walks out onto a thin bit of rock jutting out from the cliff-face. It offers him a view down into the valley and to the place where Chuzir and the women are waiting for him. They are well-hidden by the trees, so he cannot see them. From where he is standing, he can see a thin ridge of cliffs that he was not able to see from the woods that morning, and although this new path might involve some slightly dangerous climbing, it would allow him to gain several hours. Sarantuya had told him to get a move on[3], after all, and he has learned to follow her advice over the years. Even though Sarantuya does get a little mystifying with all her oracling[4], she has never led him down the wrong path. Well, except that one time, maybe.

Whilst this shortcut[5] is just as tiring and dangerous as he expected, he is actually making faster progress[6]. He even thinks that he can get back to the others as much as an hour before sundown, perhaps even earlier than that.

A good hour before this, he reaches an upright piece of rock about the height of a man. He climbs up on it to get his bearings[7] and then realises that his luck has run out[8].

He still cannot see the encampment[9], nor can he make out[10] any smoke. He has warned Arbesa not to make a fire, despite the cold, to avoid being

1 **betrayal** - *Betrug*
2 **descent** - *Abstieg*
3 **to get a move on** - *sich sputen*
4 **oracling** - *Orakeln*
5 **shortcut** - *Schleichweg*
6 **to make progress** - *vorankommen*
7 **to get one's bearings** - *sich orientieren, sich einen Überblick verschaffen*
8 **his luck has run out** - *sein Glückssträhne ist zu Ende*
9 **encampment** - *Lagerplatz*
10 **to make out** - *erkennen*

seen by their trackers, but then he looks out to the plain they came across and sees a good dozen little black dots moving towards their camp.

It is the Tajin. They've found their trail and are following it to the camp.

Timucin does not allow himself to be afraid, but forces himself to look at the situation like a warrior. Like the warrior he has become, despite his young years. The black dots are too far away to recognise them properly[1], or even work out in which direction exactly they are headed. Nevertheless, he does not doubt for a second that they are Tajin warriors. They must be.

Instead of wasting any more time thinking about things, he climbs down and sets off even faster than before. He takes several falls[2] and is completely exhausted when he reaches their makeshift[3] camp, limping[4], his hands and elbows badly scratched and bloody[5].

Arbesa has probably heard his steps and runs towards him, throwing her arms around his neck[6].

"You're back! Praise Tenghis[7], you're back! What did you find up there?"

Timucin gently moves out of her embrace[8] and pushes her away from him slightly, even though her presence[9] warms his heart.

"There's no time for that now," he says, "we have to leave. Quickly!"

Arbesa goes even paler[10] than she already is, but she is as sharp as ever: "The Tajin?"

"Yes, and they'll be here any moment now. Quickly!"

1 **properly** – *wirklich, zünftig, recht*
2 **to take a fall** – *stürzen*
3 **makeshift** – *provisorisch*
4 **to limp** – *humpeln*
5 **bloody** – *blutig*
6 **to throw one's arms around sb.'s neck** – *jdm. um den Hals fallen*
7 **praise Tenghis!** – *Tenghis sei dank!*
8 **embrace** – *Umarmung*
9 **presence** – *Gegenwart*
10 **pale** – *blass*

Without saying another word, Arbesa turns and takes the last few steps to the encampment, passing through a rampant[1] bush with her slim body. He is relieved to find Üdschin not just awake, but on her feet and already packing her few remaining possessions[2]. Perhaps she has heard a little of the conversation and has done just the right thing, as Timucin knows she always does.

He can't see Chuzir, though.

"Where is Chuzir?"

"He went off a couple of hours ago," answers Arbesa, bending down[3] to shake the snow off of the blanket she and Üdschin have been sitting on.

"He said he was going to get some fresh water and to keep an eye out for[4] the Tajin. He said he would be back now, actually."

"Get water?" says Timucin to make sure[5]. They were not running low on water when he left, and Chuzir promised to look after Arbesa and his mother until he got back. A horrible thought starts to spread in his mind, but he tries to ignore it. "Come on, quickly now."

Arbesa wants to say something else, but he is in no mood to hear it. He cuts her off with a gesture and helps her to pack all of her possessions onto the horses. It does not take long, because they do not have much left. By force of habit, Üdschin starts to erase her traces[6], but he stops her doing this immediately. Their trackers already know where they are. With one of their horses in the one hand and his mother's hand in the other, he starts off for the edge of the forest.

There are just a few steps left to go, but Timucin starts to wonder if it isn't already too late. The riders are now so close that he can see the colours of the pennants[7] on their spears. They are Tajin, no question, and

1 **rampant** – *wuchernd*
2 **possession** – *Habseligkeit*
3 **to bend down** – *sich bücken*
4 **to keep an eye out for sb.** – *nach jdm. Ausschau halten*
5 **to make sure** – *sich vergewissern*
6 **to erase one's traces** – *seine Spuren verwischen*
7 **pennant** – *Wimpel*

they are no longer trying to hide themselves or move carefully, but are coming as fast as the difficult terrain[1] will let them.

"It's over," whispers Üdschin, "they are going to catch us."

Timucin would love to contradict her, but how? There are well over a dozen Tajin warriors hunting them, and there is nowhere to hide anywhere near. On his left, he becomes aware of[2] a narrow gully[3] in which they will be able to ride faster and gain on their pursuers[4]. He doesn't know where the gully leads, or if it leads anywhere. The worst of it all is that, in order to get there, he will have to ride some distance towards the enemy warriors. But there is no choice!

The first part of the ground is too steep[5] to ride, so they have to pull their horses along behind them. Üdschin falls twice, and although the swampy[6] ground is soft and she does not hurt herself, he realises just how weak his mother still is. They have yet to reach the gully as his mother says the words he has been dreading[7] for some time.

"You have to leave me here; I'm just holding you up. If you leave me here, you might be able to escape[8] them."

Timucin does not answer at all, but just tries to pull the shying[9] pony along behind him even faster than before. At the same time, he looks up to the Tajin and then almost wishes he hadn't: the enemy warriors have come a lot closer. While they may be without honour, the Tajin are not without intelligence, and they know why they are headed for the gully. So they are making their horses gallop even faster.

Suddenly, it looks as if fate may have changed its mind and decided to give them another chance, or to at least stretch out this cruel[10] game.

1 **terrain** – *Boden, Gelände*
2 **to become aware of sth.** – *etw. gewahren*
3 **gully** – *Schlucht*
4 **to gain on one's pursuers** – *seinen Vorsprung ausbauen*
5 **steep** – *steil, abschüssig*
6 **swampy** – *sumpfig*
7 **to dread sth.** – *sich vor etw. fürchten*
8 **to escape** – *entkommen*
9 **shying** – *scheuend*
10 **cruel** – *grausam*

They are now making better progress, whilst their pursuers[1] are suddenly having trouble. They are slowing down as if they are stuck in a swamp or in quicksand[2]. Their horses plod,[3] putting one hoof slowly in front of the other. Timucin does not dare to hope that they will be so lucky, but he is not going to let this chance slip by. He drags the horse and Üdschin the last few steps of the way, reaches solid[4] ground and then lets go of the reins[5] so that he can hurry back to help Arbesa the last few steps of the way.

He looks over to the enemy and sees that things are getting more and more difficult for them. Many of their horses appear to be stuck[6] and, just as he is looking over, one of the riders falls from the saddle. Timucin is not naive[7] enough to believe that the Tajin will be stuck there forever, but if they keep moving this slowly, he and the women will actually be able to escape.

TR. 07

He turns back and his courage sinks back just as his hope was getting up. His horses are emaciated[8], exhausted by far too many months of privation. No matter how much of a lead[9] they build up now, there will be no way of escaping the fast, powerful and well-rested[10] animals that the Tajin have, especially as one of the horses will have to carry two.

As if she is reading his thoughts, his mother repeats her plea[11]:

"Go on without me, we have one horse too few!"

He is about to answer, but Arbesa is quicker:

1 **pursuer** – *Verfolger*
2 **quicksand** – *Treibsand*
3 **to plod** – *trotten, sich dahinschleppen, sich abmühen*
4 **solid** – *fest*
5 **reins** – *Zügel*
6 **to be stuck** – *feststecken*
7 **naive** – *naiv*
8 **emaciated** – *abgemagert*
9 **lead** – *Vorsprung*
10 **well-rested** – *ausgeruht*
11 **plea** – *Bitte*

"We will *not* leave you behind! If the gods are on our side, we will escape!"

The gods? Timucin is about to laugh, but then again, maybe not the gods.

Sarantuya! he thinks, desperately. *Help me!* He waits for something to stir[1] in him, for the huge power of the dragon to stream through him[2] and enable him to just turn around and pulverise[3] his enemies. Yet nothing happened. Sarantuya is silent. In fact, she is so absent that it is as if she never existed.

"We will take turns riding in pairs. The horses are strong, they will carry us!" says Arbesa. That is, however, just what they will not do, thinks Timucin sadly. In fact, if they do as Arbesa suggests, the Tajin will catch them and take them prisoner – or worse.

As horrifying[4] as it may be, Timucin's mother is right: they have one horse too few and one of them will have to stay behind.

"Leave me here," says Üdschin, "I will try to hold them up[5]."

Timucin is silent for a moment, for one single, but somehow endless moment. Then he reaches a decision which stabs at his heart like a glowing[6] dagger[7] and for which he knows he will never be able to forgive[8] himself, even if he should live to be one hundred years old.

Without a word, he goes to one of the horses, swings himself up into the saddle and then brings the animal next to the other pony so that he can reach out to both Arbesa and his mother.

"Forgive me," he whispers.

1 **to stir** – *sich regen*
2 **to stream through sb.** – *jdn. durchströmen*
3 **pulverise** – *zerschmettern*
4 **horrifying** – *grausam*
5 **to hold sb. up** – *jdn. aufhalten*
6 **glowing** – *glühend*
7 **dagger** – *Dolch*
8 **to forgive** – *vergeben, verzeihen*

It is so painful: the look of utter confusion[1] in Arbesa's eyes, the complete astonishment[2] as he reaches out and pulls his mother – and not Arbesa – up onto the empty saddle of the second pony.

He gallops off. Üdschin's horse lets out a shrill[3] cry. Although he doesn't look back, he thinks he can see Arbesa standing there, turning round to stare at him and Üdschin wide-eyed with disbelief[4]. Üdschin screams something that he neither understands nor wants to hear. She tries weakly to reach for the reins to stop the horse, but Timucin gives the horse a slap and it speeds up even more.

In fact, the gods appear to be on their side. As he looks round – carefully avoiding Arbesa – he can see that the Tajin are still having difficulty advancing[5]. With every step, their lead is growing.

In front of them, the gully splits off into several little valleys, and these then split into a kind of labyrinth that could hide an entire army, let alone[6] two riders. Moreover, the ground is hard and dry, so they barely leave a trace.

Timucin asks himself if the gods are perhaps playing a particularly cruel game with him in allowing them to escape against all odds[7] so that he could have an entire lifetime to brood over[8] his horrible crime[9].

Then he wonders if it isn't the gods that are sending him these thoughts, but Sarantuya. Nevertheless, he keeps the horses galloping, into another gully, into another valley, further over rocky peaks and then into a deep valley.

He would almost certainly keep going further and further, but the horses begin to fail. His own animal starts to shy and then just stops. Üd-

1 **utter confusion** – *völlige Fassungslosigkeit*
2 **astonishment** – *Erstaunen*
3 **shrill** – *schrill*
4 **wide-eyed with disbelief** – *mit ungläubig aufgerissenen Augen*
5 **to advance** – *vorankommen, sich vorwärts bewegen*
6 **let alone** – *geschweige denn*
7 **against all odds** – *entgegen aller Wahrscheinlichkeit*
8 **to brood over sth** – *über etw. brüten, nachdenken*
9 **crime** – *Frevel*

schin's horse also stops at this moment before it collapses[1] on its front legs. Üdschin slips off its back, but manages to stay standing and not fall over.

In one swift movement,[2] Timucin is next to her to help her. She shakes off[3] his hand and flashes her eyes at him[4] so strongly that he takes a step back.

"What have you done?" she screams at him: "Have you gone mad? You have left your future wife to save a haggard crone[5]! Is that the kind of honour I taught you? Do you wish to bring shame on yourself and on your tribe?"

"You are not a crone, but my mother," answers Timucin. *You will betray the one you love the most.* "They won't do anything to Arbesa."

Üdschin laughs at this.

"Why? Because they are such men of honour?"

"They will not do anything," insists[6] Timucin, mainly to convince himself, "for they may be cruel and dishonourable[7], but they are not stupid. Arbesa's father is the khan of the Voshon. He would exterminate[8] their entire clan if they so much as cut a hair off her head."

That sounds desperate, even to him. Üdschin simply snorts her disapproval.

"He would, yes, if he ever finds out. But he won't, and your betrothed is a pretty girl. She may not yet be a woman, but that is more than enough for the Tajin."

Timucin does not want to understand what she means. He would not be able to bear[9] the truth. Instead, he turns round roughly and goes to take a look at the horses. He forbids[10] himself to think about Arbesa.

1 **to collapse** – *zusammenbrechen*
2 **in one swift movement** – *in einem Satz*
3 **to shake off** – *abschütteln*
4 **to flash one's eyes at sb.** – *jdn. anfunkeln*
5 **haggard crone** – *ausgezehrtes altes Weib*
6 **to insist** – *beharren*
7 **dishonourable** – *ehrlos*
8 **to exterminate** – *auslöschen*
9 **to bear** – *ertragen*
10 **to forbid** – *verbieten*

One day, you will betray her, but she will forgive you.

Yet would he be able to forgive himself for what he has done?

Both horses are clearly about to collapse. Their flanks[1] are trembling; they are not able to stand still. A kind of flaky[2] white foam[3] is dripping out of their mouths and nostrils[4]. They will not be fit to ride for some time.

"We must go on. They are probably still looking for us," says Timucin.

"I shall not run away like a coward and leave my future daughter-in-law in the hands of these animals," says Üdschin decidedly, "I shall stay here."

"That is not going to save Arbesa," answers Timucin, "and her sacrifice would achieve nothing."

"*Her* sacrifice?" asks Üdschin.

Timucin wants to answer, but it is as if his throat has been sewn up[5] and he cannot speak. His eyes start to burn and become moist[6]; then he shakes his head angrily, goes over to the horses and grabs their reins. They snort and try to resist[7] him, but they are too weak even for that.

"We must go on," he says and walks off without even looking back at Üdschin. He almost doesn't care if[8] she follows him or not, and he doesn't really care anymore if the Tajin riders arrive now to finish what they started a year back.

He has nothing left to lose. They have taken his family and his future, and now he has just thrown away the last thing he had: his honour.

Üdschin is following him, as the sound of her feet dragging betrays. He does not look back because he would not be able to stand her reproachful look, but he is deeply relieved[9] that she is following. He was not entirely sure she would.

1 **flank** – *Flanke*
2 **flaky** – *flockig*
3 **foam** – *Schaum*
4 **nostrils** – *Nüstern*
5 **to sew up** – *zuschnüren*
6 **moist** – *feucht*
7 **to resist sb.** – *sich jdm. widersetzen*
8 **he doesn't care if…** – *es ist ihm gleich, ob…*
9 **relieved** – *erleichtert*

They drag themselves along[1] for about half an hour before it starts to get dark. Timucin is happy, because it will increase their chances of escaping their pursuers. As well known as the Tajin may be as hunters and trackers, not even they can see in the dark.

DRACHENFRAGE

In this chapter, Timucin has to decide whether to save Arbesa or his mother and he chooses his mother Üdschin. Is she happy about his decision?

However, he too cannot see without light, which becomes clearer and clearer to him as they reach an impassable[2] field of boulders[3] about an hour after sunset. The rocks block off the way out of the valley into which they have walked.

He is about to panic, but he keeps control of himself and forces himself to carry an optimistic expression on his face. He turns round and looks at his mother closely for the first time in a while.

"We need to find another path," he says, "there are enough of them here."

"And then?" asks Üdschin. Timucin looks at her confused.

"Then?"

"Then," repeats Üdschin, "for even if we escape, there is still the question of what to do then. Do we keep running? For how long? Where to?"

He does not answer and his mother continues speaking in a voice which is at once full of contempt[4] and yet horrifyingly empty.

"Even if you succeed in escaping, as the great khan of a tribe consisting of you and your mother, where will you go? How far do you want to flee something you cannot hide from?"

How far do you want to flee from the shame? She doesn't say this, but she doesn't need to, either.

Without a word, Timucin holds the reins of his pony even tighter and turns round in order to walk back out of the narrow valley. As he comes

1 **to drag oneself along** – *sich dahinschleppen*
2 **impassable** – *unpassierbar*
3 **boulder** – *Geröll*
4 **contempt** – *Verachtung*

out of it, he is finally convinced that the gods of fate[1] have a very black sense of humour.

There is a kind of hollow[2] in front of them with steep walls and two exits. One is very far in the distance, whilst the silhouettes of three riders are blocking the other.

Timucin's thoughts clash[3] for a second, and then he leaps[4] into the saddle of one horse, yanks Üdschin onto the back of the second one, and overcomes the weak protests of the exhausted horse with a brutal movement. A cry rings out behind them. It seems more disbelieving than angry, but then he hears the hammering of hooves[5] on stone. Someone calls something. His name?

Timucin is certain that this flight is useless, but it is the only thing he can do. His horse races off as he slaps Üdschin's pony hard on the rump[6]. It gives out a frightened neigh[7] and starts off. In sheer[8] desperation, he reaches for his bow and lays one of his three remaining arrows on the string[9].

Perhaps the gods really are on his side, perhaps Sarantuya is guiding his hand, or perhaps it is just luck. But galloping at full speed and aiming behind him[10] he manages to hit one of the riders in the thigh[11], sending him falling out of the saddle with a shout.

His second arrow, however, misses and so he is only left with the one, single, most precious arrow. He hesitates to draw it from his quiver, and perhaps too long or perhaps just long enough to stop something even worse from happening.

1 **gods of fate** – *Schicksalsgötter*
2 **hollow** – *Talkessel*
3 **to clash** – *sich überschlagen*
4 **to leap** – *springen*
5 **hoof** – *Huf*
6 **rump** – *Hinterteil*
7 **neigh** – *Wiehern*
8 **sheer** – *schier*
9 **string** – *Sehne*
10 **aiming behind him** – *hinter sich zielend*
11 **thigh** – *Schenkel*

He draws the string back as the two riders reach him. Timucin's eyes widen with pure horror[1] as he recognises one of them.

"What is...?" he gasps[2]. Something hits him so hard that he falls from the saddle. He loses consciousness[3] before he hits the ground.

1 **horror** – *Entsetzen*
2 **to gasp** – *keuchen*
3 **consciousness** – *Bewusstsein*

The Broken Oath

TR. 08

The dragon did not come to him this time, probably because he has not been asleep, but completely unconscious. He has been in a black abyss[1] where nothing can reach him. The only thing he can remember from this deep, dark place is an overwhelming[2] feeling of loneliness[3]. Not even Sarantuya could reach him there, and Timucin asks himself if the blackness[4] was not a foretaste[5] of death. If it was, then he has every reason to fear it even more.

Once Timucin has finished thinking this, several things happen at once. He feels himself waking up. It is like emerging[6] from a pool of utter darkness into a world of sounds and voices that he has trouble understanding at first. Then he feels a sharp pain, a pain that is only bearable[7] in the first few instants. As soon as he fully awake, the pain is so horrendous[8] that it seems to be splitting his skull[9] in two. He moans and is awake. Memories of the final moments come back to him in a sudden, explosive moment.

"You may open your eyes, Khan. I know that you are awake."

This voice is not unknown, but Timucin refuses to recognise it, for it will turn his horrible suspicion[10] into a far more horrible reality. He opens his eyes slightly, but then closes them immediately. The light is like a thin, white-hot[11] needle. He hears steps, and then there is the sound of a tent being closed as the red flash on his tightly-closed eyelids[12] fades.

1 **abyss** – *Abgrund*
2 **overwhelming** – *gewaltig, überwältigend*
3 **loneliness** – *Einsamkeit*
4 **blackness** – *Schwärze*
5 **foretaste** – *Vorgeschmack*
6 **to emerge from sth.** – *aus etw. auftauchen, aus etw. herauskommen*
7 **bearable** – *erträglich*
8 **horrendous** – *entsetzlich, grauenhaft*
9 **skull** – *Schädel*
10 **suspicion** – *Verdacht*
11 **white-hot** – *weißglühend*
12 **tightly-closed eyelids** – *zusammengepresste Augenlider*

Steps approach again and a bowl of cool, refreshing water is put to his lips. He drinks in deep, greedy[1] gulps[2]. He tries to grasp the bowl, but for some reason he cannot move his hands. His head still hurts appallingly[3]. He keeps drinking until the bowl is removed[4] and then opens his eyes for a second time, more carefully. The stabbing[5] light has been shut out of the yurt and he can see shadows and slightly blurred[6] outlines[7]. He realises that he can only see with his left eye. His right eye is covered with his own blood, which has dried to a crust on the right-hand side of his face. It is tight and it itches[8].

Timucin blinks a few times, although it hurts, and the big outline before his eyes becomes a face, a face he knows all too well[9]. His heart is heavy. He is not angry, but feels a mixture of disbelief[10], horror and deep sadness.

"Do you want some more water?"

Instead of answering, Timucin tries once again to move his hands. He can't, so he turns his head carefully. It hurts, something is scratching at his neck and a heavy weight is loaded on his shoulders, pulling his torso[11] forward.

He is wearing a large, wooden yoke[12] around his neck. His hands too are locked at shoulder-height.

"Are you hungry? I can bring you something to eat."

Timucin does not answer, but turns his head carefully and painfully back to the face above him.

1 **greedy** – *gierig*
2 **gulp** – *Schluck*
3 **appallingly** – *entsetzlich, furchtbar*
4 **to remove** – *zurücknehmen, entnehmen*
5 **stabbing** – *stechend*
6 **blurred** – *verschwommen*
7 **outline** – *Umriss*
8 **to itch** – *jucken*
9 **all too well** – *nur zu gut*
10 **disbelief** – *Unglauben*
11 **torso** – *Oberkörper*
12 **wooden yoke** – *hölzernes Joch (wie es Ochsen beim Ziehen eines Wagens auf den Schultern tragen)*

"Can you at least tell me why you did it?"

"I had no choice," answers Chuzir, "and believe me, Timucin, that if it had been no more than a question of my own life, I would not have hesitated to die for you[1]. But they took my father and my brother as hostages[2], and my mother and sisters too."

"And they threatened to kill them if you did not betray me to them," replies Timucin. He tries to find at least a trace of anger, but he can only muster[3] sorrow.

"I am your brother in oath, I know, and I should not have done it. But they left me no choice. If you wish it of me[4], I shall take my own life."

Timucin feels that Chuzir means these words quite seriously, and he starts to smile. He is not angry at his friend, and he certainly does not want him to die.

"No," he says, "if you owe me anything, then promise me that I will die by your hand[5]."

Chuzir is silent. Even in the pale light, Timucin can see tears on his cheeks[6], and he feels nothing but pity for his friend. He suddenly realises that his brother in oath too is in chains[7]. He may not be wearing a yoke like Timucin, and his chains may be invisible, but they are just as strong and just as painful.

"That really was a very moving speech[8] you gave there," says a scornful voice. Timucin suddenly becomes aware that they are not alone. Steps approach and he turns his head slowly. A shadow is moving towards him and splits into two outlines as it comes nearer. A second later, he recognises faces, and the embers[9] of anger start to burn in him again. He

1 **I would not have hesistated to die for you** – *ich hätte nicht gezögert, für dich zu sterben*
2 **hostages** – *Geißeln*
3 **to muster** – *aufbringen, zusammennehmen*
4 **if you wish it of me...** – *wenn du es so willst, werde ich...*
5 **by your hand** – *von deiner Hand*
6 **cheek** – *Wange*
7 **in chains** – *gefesselt*
8 **very moving speech** – *herzergreifende Rede*
9 **embers** – *Glut*

throws himself against his wooden bonds[1] with all his might, but only for a moment before it starts to hurt too much.

Tedschen is looking down at him[2], his eyes cold and hard. Tedschen, Ilhan's father, the traitor[3] who started the rebellion against Timucin and his mother. He makes no secret of[4] how much pleasure[5] Timucin's pain gives him.

"Nevertheless, I fear that I shall be unable to grant you this wish[6]," says the man who has stolen his clan and his whole life. He laughs horribly and his son Ilhan joins in the cackling[7].

"Get on your knees!" shouts Timucin. "You are both standing before your Khan!"

Ilhan stops laughing and lifts his hand ready to hit Timucin, but his father holds him back with a quick movement.

"I should very much like to, yet a khan does not kneel before someone of your young age."

"You are no khan," answers Timucin, "you are a thief[8]!"

Again, Ilhan wants to hit Timucin, and again his father stops him by hitting Timucin himself. It hurts a lot, but he simply blinks the pain away[9].

"Just kill me," he says, "or does it warm your cold heart to hit young boys in chains?"

"I should like nothing more than[10] to kill you, my boy, but I'm afraid that I am not allowed to," answers Tedschen. Nevertheless, he draws his

1 **bonds** – *Fessel*
2 **to look down at sb.** – *auf jdn. herabsehen*
3 **traitor** – *Verräter*
4 **he makes no secret of...** – *er macht kein Hehl aus...*
5 **pleasure** – *Vergnügen*
6 **to grant sb. a wish** – *jdm. einen Wunsch erfüllen*
7 **cackling** – *Gegacker*
8 **thief** – *Dieb*
9 **to blink sth. away** – *etw. wegblinzeln*
10 **I should like nothing more than to...** – *nichts täte ich lieber, als...*

sword and swings it so close to Timucin's head that it cuts a hair and thuds into[1] something behind him.

"You should take another sip of aykol," says Timucin, "and then you'll strike better." He can see in Tedschen's eyes that he would like nothing more than to do it, but he sheathes[2] his sword: "I shall kill you, but only once you are old enough to defend yourself."

"But you'll never kill him then!" says Ilhan mockingly[3].

"I have promised your friend that much," continues Tedschen, "and I shall keep to my word. When you have become a real man, I shall challenge[4] you and then kill you in a fair fight." He turns away to Chuzir. "Now, say goodbye to your friend. We are leaving soon."

Without saying anything else, he goes. Ilhan follows him, but stops at the entrance to the tent to throw Timucin a look of gleeful anticipation[5]. Timucin realises that the coming years are going to be long and arduous[6].

He is not afraid, but grimly determined[7]. They can torture[8] and hit and degrade[9] him as much as they like. He will use every punch[10], every little humiliation[11] as a source of power[12] for his revenge.

"What has happened to Arbesa," he asks, "and to my mother?"

Chuzir is silent just long enough for Timucin to become worried.

"They are going to sell Arbesa," he says, "because the Merkits have offered a high price for her."

"Have you spoken with her? Has she said anything about me?"

1 **to thud into sth.** – *in etw. dumpf einschlagen*
2 **to sheathe a sword** – *sein Schwert einstecken*
3 **mockingly** – *spöttisch*
4 **to challenge sb.** – *jdn. fordern*
5 **gleeful anticipation** – *hämische Vorfreude*
6 **arduous** – *angestrengt, mühsam*
7 **grimly determined** – *grimmig entschlossen*
8 **to torture sb.** – *jdn. quälen*
9 **to degrade sb.** – *erniedrigen*
10 **punch** – *Faustschlag*
11 **humiliation** – *Demütigung, Erniedrigung*
12 **source of power** – *Kraftquelle*

Chuzir shakes his head silently, but this is no comfort[1]. Timucin would almost like his brother in oath to reproach[2] him.

"What about my mother?"

"The Tajin did nothing to her," replies Chuzir, "but nobody wants to pay a ransom for her. I think Tedschen is going to allow me to take her with me. I cannot offer her much, but she will live."

"And do you think that either Tedschen or Ilhan are just going to let you go?"

"I am not stupid," answers Chuzir, "and I know too much that he does not want other people to find out. Something bad might happen to me[3]. But don't worry, I'll be careful."

He goes silent. For a while, neither Timucin nor Chuzir know what to say.

"Go on, go," says Timucin, "and take care of[4] my mother. And, if you can, of..."

"... of Arbesa," promises Chuzir: "I will send someone to the Merkits. They won't do anything to her. She is a pretty young girl and her father's clan is powerful."

Timucin does not answer. He does not want to talk about Arbesa, or even think about her, not after what he has done to her[5].

"Now I must go," says Chuzir, uncomfortable[6], "but do not be afraid. Tedschen is bound to his word[7] not to do anything to you until you are a man."

"I shall try to grow slowly," answers Timucin with a quirky[8] smile. Chuzir smiles back, but both of them realise it is a charade[9].

1 **comfort** – *Trost*
2 **to reproach sb.** – *jdm. Vorwürfe machen*
3 **something bad might happen to me...** – *mir könnte etwas Schlimmes zustoßen...*
4 **to take care of sb.** – *auf jdn. Acht geben*
5 **not after what he has done to her** – *nicht nach dem, was er ihr angetan hatte*
6 **uncomfortable** – *unbehaglich*
7 **bound to his word** – *an sein Wort gebunden*
8 **quirky** – *schief*
9 **charade** – *Affentheater*

"I know one of the Tajin, he will look out for you[1]," adds Chuzir quietly. He shrugs his shoulders: "Well, if I'm honest, I bribed[2] him. It's better for you if you don't know who he is, however."

They look at each other for a long moment.

"Alright, clear off![3]" says Timucin after a while. Chuzir grins, turns and goes. Timucin briefly asks himself if that was the right way to say goodbye to a friend he might never see again, but Chuzir is already gone.

DRACHENFRAGE

Why did Chuzir, who swore an oath to protect Timucin, feel forced to betray him?

Didn't Sarantuya say that he was going to be a great ruler[4], though, whose name would be known from one end of the earth to the other? Who would be known and feared? *So doesn't that mean that you will see your brother in oath again in any case?* asks the dragon.

Instead of answering, Timucin asks a question of his own. *Why didn't you help me?* He has a vague feeling of sadness in his thoughts, but he can't say quite why or about whom. He doesn't get an answer, so he asks another question.

"Will you help me to get out of here[5]?"

Perhaps I will help you to help yourself, answers the dragon, and Timucin does not say anything back. Sarantuya now has a certain tone in her voice that he knows all too well. It does not matter one bit[6] what the actual question is and how often he asks, she is only going to poke fun at him[7] or answer in ambiguous[8] riddles[9]. He is sad and angry, because if he has ever needed the dragon's help, it is now.

1 **to look out for sb.** – *auf jdn. Acht geben*
2 **to bribe sb.** – *jdn. bestechen*
3 **clear off!** – *hau ab!*
4 **ruler** – *Herrscher*
5 **to get out of here** – *von hier zu entkommen*
6 **It does not matter one bit. (Redewendung)** – *Es ist ganz egal.*
7 **to poke fun at sb.** – *jdn. verspotten*
8 **ambigious** – *mehrdeutig*
9 **riddle** – *Rätsel*

And what do you expect me to do, little Genghis? Do you want me to burn all of the Tajin with my fiery[1] *breath?*

Why did you not warn me? Why did you let me betray Arbesa?

But I did warn you, little Genghis. It was a long time ago, but I know you haven't forgotten it.

"Yes, but not like that!" objects Timucin. It is true. Sarantuya did warn him that he would betray her. But not like that!

1 **fiery** – *feurig*

Captivity[1]

TR. 09

The tent opens and a Tajin enters. He is not particularly big, but he looks wily[2] and, in spite of the cold, is not wearing a coat, but a sleeveless[3] shirt made of soft leather that shows off his tattooed and muscular[4] arms. What show-offs these Tajin are![5] They are also utter cowards, however – and just like all cowards, they are even crueller when they get power.

Before Timucin can say anything, the Tajin picks him up and throws him out of the tent. Outside, Timucin is hit in the back even harder and he falls. The yoke stops him and he falls roughly on his side, cutting his knee and his elbow. While the wooden yoke stops him hitting his head, his neck falls over it so hard that he is winded[6] for several minutes and, bent double[7], fears that he may suffocate[8].

Finally, two strong hands yank him up to his feet so brutally that he lets out an agonised[9] shout. It helps him to start breathing again.

"Oh no, you're not going to get out of it that easily!" smirks[10] Ilhan, holding him with the one hand and punching him so hard in the stomach that he is winded again. After the third punch, he is violently sick[11] on the yoke in front of his face. Malicious[12] laughter rings out. Ilhan pushes him to his knees but keeps one hand in his hair so that he doesn't fall to the ground.

1 **captivity** – *Gefangenschaft*
2 **wily** – *verschlagen, gerissen*
3 **sleeveless** – *ärmellos*
4 **muscular** – *muskulös*
5 **What show-offs these Tajin are!** – *Sie sind furchtbare Angeber, diese Tajin!*
6 **winded** – *atemlos, nach Atem ringend*
7 **to bend double** – *sich krümmen*
8 **suffocate** – *ersticken*
9 **agonised** – *gequält*
10 **to smirk** – *höhnisch grinsen*
11 **to be violently sick** – *sich qualvoll erbrechen*
12 **malicious** – *hämisch, schadenfroh*

"Did you think you could just slip out[1] of here, oh mighty Khan?" says Ilhan scornfully, once again to more laughter from the Tajin, who have gathered in a circle, jeering[2] loudly as if waiting for a fight.

"Go on... hit... me," says Timucin painfully, "and if you're feeling daring[3], you might want to let me out of this yoke first. Or are you afraid?"

For a moment, Ilhan's face is full of hatred[4]. Timucin can see nothing in his eyes except the desire to kill him. He clenches his fist[5] and then lets his arm sink back down. A wicked[6] grin spreads across his face.

"Oh yes, I almost forgot that nobody's allowed to touch you," he snorts, "you are still under the protection of the khan, after all. But I shall keep an eye on you[7], you mark my word[8]. Nothing will happen to you until you have become a man, and the years until you are will be long, very long, that I promise you!"

He gives Timucin another punch, sending him flying[9] onto his back, but stops there and leaves Timucin to the approving[10] laughter of the Tajin. Timucin stays on the ground for a while and waits for something to happen. Finally, the same warrior who threw him out of the tent a few moments ago pulls him back to his feet and, although he is not nearly as rough[11] as Ilhan, pushes him along so violently that he has trouble[12] in not falling over again.

The Tajin camp is little more than a handful of simple yurts set up in a narrow valley. There is little protection against the wind or the cold,

1 **to slip out** – *sich davonstehlen*
2 **to jeer** – *johlen*
3 **daring** – *tollkühn*
4 **Ilhan's face is full of hatred** – *Ilhans Gesicht verzerrt sich vor Hass*
5 **to clench one's fist** – *die Hand zur Faust ballen*
6 **wicked** – *niederträchtig*
7 **to keep an eye on sb.** – *jdn. im Auge behalten*
8 **you mark my word (Redewendung)** – *mein Wort darauf*
9 **to send sb. flying** – *jdn. zum Boden schleudern*
10 **approving** – *beifällig*
11 **rough** – *grob*
12 **to have trouble doing sth.** – *Mühe haben, etw. zu machen*

and the horses are stabled[1] in a makeshift pen[2]. There are some sheep and about half a dozen pigs that the warriors have probably brought by way of supplies[3]. Timucin is not surprised as he is led there and then thrown into the muddy[4] pool[5]. His yoke is bound to a heavy wooden post[6] by means of an iron chain.

DRACHENFRAGE

Why does Tedschen not kill Timucin as soon as he is captured?

"Don't run off anywhere!" says his guard[7] with smirks and jeers: "Go and say hello to your new friends. You'll be spending a lot of time together."

Timucin does not do them the favour of[8] begging or crying, although he wants to. He fixes his captor[9] with a dark stare, and slips around[10] a little in the cold mud until he has found the most comfortable position he can – well, it is the least uncomfortable position. The warrior stays there for a while and seems to be waiting for Timucin to say or do something that will give him reason to hit him. Eventually[11], he shrugs his shoulders and walks off.

Two pigs come over to sniff[12] their new penmate[13]. Timucin waits until they are close enough before kicking the bigger of the two animals on its curious[14], sniffing nose. He probably hasn't even hurt the animal, but the

1 **to stable a horse** – *ein Pferd unterbringen*
2 **pen** – *Pferch*
3 **supplies** – *Proviant*
4 **muddy** – *schlammig*
5 **pool** – *Suhle*
6 **post** – *Pfosten*
7 **guard** – *Wächter*
8 **to do sb. the favour of doing sth.** – *jdm. einen Gefallen tun*
9 **captor** – *Fänger*
10 **to slip around** – *hin- und herrutschen*
11 **eventually** – *schließlich, endlich*
12 **to sniff sb.** – *jdn. beschnüffeln*
13 **penmate** – *Mitbewohner im Pferch*
14 **curious** – *neugierig*

kick was hard enough for the pig to run away with a frightened squeak[1], and the second animal follows.

Timucin struggles slightly as he sinks back down into the icy mud, keeping his eye on the pigs for a few moments. Although pigs are useful animals and far more intelligent than most people think, they can also be more dangerous than most would assume[2]. So he takes some time to make sure that the pigs are keeping a respectful distance and then risks a look around the camp.

The warriors have already begun taking down their tents. They are skilled and fast, like all men who have grown up on the Mongolian steppe. Their yurts seem to disappear in a blink of an eye[3], loaded onto packhorses[4] or simple two-wheeled carts[5]. Other horses are being saddled[6] ready to leave.

Timucin is surprised by the number of Tajin. He knew they were being followed by a large number of warriors, but there are more than twice as many men here as his father's clan counted before. Had all of these men being looking for him for almost a year? Why?

Because they are afraid of you, little Genghis.

"Rubbish!" says Timucin out loud[7]. The pig he has just kicked looks over at him and squeaks reproachfully. Timucin continues to speak, more quietly. "Why should they be afraid of me? I am just one person and the only warrior left in my clan!"

Yet the blood of a khan flows in your veins[8]. Sometimes people can feel things coming, and although they do not know what is coming, they are afraid.

1 **squeak** – *Quieken*
2 **more dangerous than most would assume** – *gefährlicher als man gemeinhin annimmt*
3 **in a blink of an eye** – *im Handumdrehen*
4 **packhorse** – *Packpferd*
5 **cart** – *Karre*
6 **to saddle a horse** – *ein Pferd satteln*
7 **to say sth. out loud** – *etw. laut sagen*
8 **vein** – *Ader, Vene*

"Afraid?" Timucin wants to laugh, but he is too weak. The pig is looking at him more and more distrustfully[1], and starts sniffing towards him: it draws back as soon as he raises his foot. "Afraid? Who is going to be afraid of a boy chained up with pigs?"

The pigs? answers Sarantuya, amused at her own wit[2], before returning to a more serious tone: *Perhaps they can feel the dragon in you, little Genghis?*

"So why don't they just kill me then?" Strangely enough[3], the thought is not as frightening as it might seem.

Maybe they feel your power, but know as little as you about what will become of it[4].

"Do you know, then?"

Am I mistaken[5]*, or have you not already asked me that once before?*

"I did, but you did not answer."

And what makes you think I will now?

He is not in the mood for one of Sarantuya's duels of words, and is about to answer curtly when he sees something that instantly makes him forget both the dragon and his unfortunate[6] situation.

The camp is almost ready to leave, but it will take them at least another hour to actually ride off, and not all of them will be riding. Timucin sees four horses trotting[7] past at some distance to his pig prison, three being ridden by Tajin and one carrying a much smaller figure with chained[8] hands. It is Arbesa.

Her face can hardly be seen under the furry hood[9], yet Timucin sees enough to notice that she is pale and exhausted. She seems to be having

1 **distrustful** – *misstrauisch*
2 **wit** – *Witz*
3 **strangely enough** – *komischerweise*
4 **...what will become of it** – *...was daraus werden wird*
5 **to be mistaken** – *sich täuschen, sich irren*
6 **unfortunate** – *misslich, unglücklich*
7 **to trot** – *traben*
8 **chained** – *gefesselt*
9 **hood** – *Kapuze*

difficulty not falling asleep in the saddle. If she just lifts her head, she will see him, but she seems to be too tired or too dispirited[1] to do so.

Timucin is about to call her name so that she looks over. At least he'll be able to see her beautiful face and beguiling[2] eyes one more time. Then, however, he remembers what she will see: a half-naked boy, bleeding, tied up with the pigs and locked in a yoke stained[3] with his own vomit.

No – Timucin would give his eye-teeth[4] to look at her one more time-but he does not want her to see him like this, for *this* to be her last memory of him.

He watches her go by, silently, until his eyes are so full of tears that he cannot see anything any more. They will not see each other again for a long time.

1 **dispirited** – *mutlos*
2 **beguiling** – *betörend*
3 **to stain** – *beflecken, besudeln*
4 **he would give his eye-teeth to do sth.** – *er würde seinen rechten Arm dafür geben, etw. zu tun*

Flight[1]

TR. 10

The Tajin are arming themselves for war[2]. It is the fourth or fifth war they have fought since Timucin has been with them. As is their way[3], they feast on the night before they leave, drinking themselves into unconsciousness[4]. Perhaps this is the chance he has been waiting five years for.

It will have to be, for he will not get another. He is almost a man now, and he already expected Tedschen to come to his jailor[5] last summer and ask him to release Timucin for their man-to-man combat[6]. Instead, however, Tedschen's son Ilhan came, himself almost grown into a man, and certainly a lot bigger and stronger than Timucin. He examined Timucin and then went back to the tribe they stole from him. Nothing happened. Yet Timucin is not foolish enough to believe that Tedschen has forgotten his vow[7] to come and kill him as soon as he is a man.

Timucin is not afraid of death. In fact, he has often wished for it in the last few years. Whenever he has been beaten, tortured or humiliated[8], he has wished for it. Sometimes he has even thought of bringing death to himself, for each day has come with new horrors, new pains and new degradations[9]: the Tajin are clever when it comes to thinking of new ways to harry[10] him.

He would have done it too, if he had not had this picture of hope in his mind: Arbesa's exhausted face and her empty eyes as he last saw her five years ago, on that morning on which she was taken away. All this

1 **flight** – *Flucht*
2 **to arm oneself for war** – *zum Krieg rüsten*
3 **as is their way** – *wie es ihre Art ist*
4 **to drink oneself into unconsciousness** – *sich bis zur Bewusstlosigkeit betrinken*
5 **jailor** – *Kerkermeister*
6 **combat** – *Kampf*
7 **vow** – *Schwur*
8 **to humiliate sb.** – *jdn. demütigen*
9 **degradation** – *Entwürdigung, Demütigung*
10 **to harry sb.** – *jdn. ständig belästigen*

time, he has not once thought of the fate that awaited her[1], and yet it is thinking of her that gives him the strength to bear all of this and more. He has sworn[2] to protect Arbesa, and he will keep to his oath[3].

DRACHENFRAGE

Why is this the last chance that Timucin will have to escape from his captivity?

"Oi, Khan of the Pigs!"

The voice cuts into his thoughts like a knife, and Timucin tenses up[4] for the punches that are sure to come.

"What are you doing standing around as if you had nothing better to do? If you've got nothing to do, we'll find something for you."

Timucin hurries to pick up the two buckets[5] and take them to the river. There is a fountain in the middle of this little village, which offers plenty of fresh water from the river. So making him go down the steep slope[6] to the river with these heavy buckets is just another form of harassment[7] – even if it is one of the more harmless ones.

With his hands still in the heavy wooden yoke, however, this task is almost impossible to complete, just like almost all other everyday[8] movements. It took him a year just to learn how to do the simplest things without knocking something over, spilling[9] something, falling over or breaking something – all of which just gave the Tajin another excuse[10] to beat him or think up a new way to punish him.

He hurries back to the celebrations with the buckets, only to find that the men do not need or want any water. It is just another little nastiness[11] thought up by Kesrit, his own personal master torturer[12].

1 **the fate that awaited her** - *das Schicksal, das sie erwartete*
2 **to swear** - *schwören*
3 **oath** - *Eid*
4 **to tense up** - *sich spannen*
5 **bucket** - *Eimer*
6 **slope** - *Böschung*
7 **harassment** - *Schikane*
8 **everyday** - *alltäglich*
9 **to spill sth.** - *etw. verschütten*
10 **excuse** - *Vorwand*
11 **nastiness** - *Bosheit*
12 **torturer** - *Folterknecht*

Timucin is careful, of course, not to show his real feelings. He sets down the buckets in the uncomfortable fashion which the yoke limits him to, without once pulling a face[1], even as one of the men kicks over the bucket, sending the icy water that he has had so much trouble getting from the river all over the floor and his bare[2] feet. All the other men laugh at this new form of malice[3], yet Timucin does not show his state of mind[4]. Instead, he notices how drunk the men already are, and it is not even midnight yet. Whoever it is they are fighting will have an easy job tomorrow.

The more important point, however, is that they will be far more drunk than usual tonight. Even Kesrit, his guard, who has not left him alone for five long years, will be very drunk. Normally, he does not drink as much as the others, but tonight he has been taking deep swigs of aykol. Since he is not as used to it[5] as the others, even a smaller amount will have a worse effect on him than on the others.

By midnight, most of the warriors have gone to sleep, and a couple of hours later the very last reveller[6] is snoring away[7] as Kesrit leads him to the little yurt on the edge of the camp that they share. Well, "share" means that Timucin sleeps on the floor. Kesrit chains him to a post and is himself snoring moments after lying down on his luxurious bed of fur and hides[8].

Timucin waits for another hour or so, weighing up[9] the arguments for and against running away against one another. He has often done this in the last five years, but has never really had to choose. Now he must. Not that there is a particular reason, but he somehow *knows* that fate has arranged this chance for him – and that there will not be a second one.

1 **to pull a face** – *die Miene verziehen*
2 **bare** – *bloß, unbedeckt, unbekleidet*
3 **malice** – *Bosheit*
4 **state of mind** – *Geisteszustand*
5 **to be used to sth.** – *etw. gewohnt sein*
6 **reveller** – *Feiernder*
7 **to snore away** – *vor sich hin schnarchen*
8 **hide** – *Fell*
9 **to weigh two things up against one another** – *zwei Sachen gegeneinander abwiegen*

He listens to Kesrit's even breathing and snoring and, as soon as he is sure that the tattooed warrior is fast asleep[1], he moves to the side and digs[2] for his most precious treasure[3]: it is a rusty, bent nail[4] that he found two years ago and has carefully guarded[5] ever since. He uses it silently and skilfully, as he has so often practised, to open the heavy lock[6] which keeps the chain in place. Without making a sound, he lets the chain slowly fall to the ground and then slowly slips out of the tent.

Now he must decide. Either he can stay, afraid of his own courage, and return to his chains as he has so often done after practising. On many nights, he has freed himself and then crept around the camp looking for the best escape route. But he has always come back to wait for the right moment. Now it has come, and if he goes now, then he is taking his life into his hands[7].

Kesrit and the other Tajin have made no bones about the fact[8] that any escape attempt will be punished with death, no matter what they may have promised Tedschen.

TR. 11

Once he has convinced himself that there can be no going back[9], he steps out of the tent once and for all[10]. He feels an immediate urge to run over to the pen, steal a horse and ride off as fast as he can. That would not just be somewhat hasty[11], but also very foolish. The yoke would not stop him from riding, but would definitely stop him from riding fast

1 **to be fast asleep** – *fest schlafen*
2 **to dig** – *graben*
3 **precious treasure** – *wertvoller Schatz*
4 **nail** – *Nagel*
5 **to guard** – *hüten*
6 **lock** – *Schloss*
7 **he is taking his life into his hands** – *dann geht es um sein Leben*
8 **to make no bones about the fact that…** – *keinen Zweifel daran lassen, dass…*
9 **there can be no going back (Redewendung)** – *es gibt kein Zurück mehr*
10 **once and for all** – *endgültig*
11 **hasty** – *übereilt, hastig*

enough to put enough distance between him and the Tajin, who will soon be on his trail.

Instead of doing this, he runs in the opposite direction straight to the middle of the village, which is made up of about four dozen yurts. Moving silently through the sleeping camp, stealing away like a shadow, he hears his father's voice explaining things to him both with patience[1] and with authority[2]. *The best plan is always the easiest one, my son. The more complicated an idea, the greater the chance you will do something wrong.* Whilst Timucin is sure his father was right, he is also very sure that he is doing the right thing now.

He goes east, taking the direction that is the least likely[3] for an escape. There is nothing except stones and rocks, not a bush or a tree, not even any water. Even the Tajin, expert trackers that they are, will have trouble following his trail here. And because they have a dispute[4] with another clan and will have to go into battle the following morning, they will not be able to spare[5] many men for the search. If Timucin can just get out of the yoke, then he will have a good chance of escaping. And although he will suffer hunger and thirst, the privations of the past years have prepared him for this, while the hard work he has been forced to do has made him strong – much stronger than the Tajin probably think.

Timucin creeps silently down the river to the spot[6] where he had already hidden two pouches with water that afternoon. On the way, he indulges in[7] revenge fantasies in which he returns as the head of a mighty army and wipes out[8] the Tajin down to the very last man.

A quiet voice inside him tells him that doing so would only make him into the torturer, because two wrongs do not make a right[9], and yet he

1 **patience** – *Geduld*
2 **authority** – *Souveränität*
3 **the least likely** – *am Unwahrscheinlichsten*
4 **dispute** – *Streit*
5 **to spare** – *entbehren, erübrigen*
6 **spot** – *Stelle*
7 **to indulge in sth.** – *sich in etw. ergehen*
8 **to wipe out** – *auslöschen*
9 **two wrongs do not make a right** – *zweimal falsch ergibt nicht einmal richtig*

would be tempted[1] to justify this evil. Nevertheless, along with thoughts of Arbesa, it is these fantasies that have kept him going[2] in the last five years. And as long as they remain fantasies, they do not harm anyone.

Are you sure of that, my little Khan?

The dragon's voice is as quiet and familiar as ever, sounding in his thoughts and nowhere else. Yet Timucin jumps[3] and almost shouts, which might well have woken people in the camp.

"Sarantuya?" he murmurs, shocked.

The dragon continues as if their last conversation had been just a few moments ago and not five years back: *It is almost always our thoughts that influence our actions, little Khan.*

"Rubbish!" answers Timucin. "And don't call me that!"

Little Genghis, continues Sarantuya, *what I mean is, to be more precise: do you not think that, if you imagine doing something long enough, it becomes easier to do it?*

Timucin does not really listen to the question, and does not want to think about it at all. Although he is answering in his head, he is almost shouting: *Where have you been all this time? Five years, Sarantuya! I haven't heard from you for five years! Did you not want anything to do with the Khan of the Pigs?*

That was the worst thing for you, wasn't it, that they called you that? replies Sarantuya. He feels the soft presence of the dragon within him, feels her calming force. It is the first time in an eternity[4]. The dragon says nothing, and Timucin once again concentrates on the here and now, taking the water pouches from their hiding place[5]. With his hands tied, it is more difficult than he expects to manoeuvre[6] them onto his back in a way that he can carry them comfortably. After just a few steps, he

1 **to be tempted** – *verführt werden*
2 **to keep sb. going** – *jdm. Kraft geben*
3 **to jump** – *erschrocken zusammenfahren*
4 **eternity** – *Ewigkeit*
5 **hiding place** – *Versteck*
6 **to manoeuvre** – *bugsieren*

realises that he has underestimated their weight. But without this water, he has no chance at all.

He wades[1] through the river and walks for a long while through the dried up grass on the other side. Then he heads for a piece of rocky ground on which he will leave no further traces. As soon as he reaches the rock, he turns back and follows his own tracks back to the river, and wades a good half mile through the icy water. He goes for as long as he can, until there is no feeling left in his feet except pain and he is stumbling[2] more than he is walking. Yet there is no time for rest. Many miles to the east, there is an area he knows where he can hide, a place of bare rocks, labyrinthine gullies and ravines[3]. At the moment, however, darkness is his only protection and the night is already old. He must hurry.

Where were you the whole time? he asks.

I was always there, little Genghis, answers the dragon, *you were never alone – and you felt that deep inside you.*

But you never talked to me, answers Timucin reproachfully.

Because it was not necessary, little Genghis, the dragon replies, *and it would not have done you any good.*

You mean because the odd bit of torture[4] *strengthens my character*[5]*?* Inside him, he hears a pleasant laugh.

I would have put it a little more diplomatically[6], *but essentially, that's right. It was time for you to learn a little humility*[7], *my Khan.*

Humility?

There was no answer, just a sound behind him. He jumps round and sees something shadowy[8], something blacker than the black night itself.

1 **to wade** – *waten*
2 **to stumble** – *stolpern*
3 **ravine** – *Hohlweg*
4 **the odd bit of torture** – *ein bisschen Folter hin und wieder*
5 **to strengthen one's character** – *den Charakter stählen*
6 **I would have put it a little more diplomatically** – *ich hätte es ein wenig diplomatischer ausgedrückt*
7 **humility** – *Demut*
8 **shadowy** – *schattig*

"Well, what a surprise!" says someone in a slightly slurred[1] voice: "Look at that: there I go down to the river to follow the call of nature[2] and who do I see? The Khan of the Pigs! What's the matter? Have you got lost[3]?"

Timucin does not bother answering. He does not need to see his face clearly to recognise Kesrit, his guard. The slow slur of his speech[4], however, is enough for Timucin so see how drunk he is, and that he is not here to exchange pleasantries[5]. He hears the sound of metal scraping on metal as the moonlight breaks on the polished steel of Kesrit's sword.

"Do you want to kill me now?" he asks, his voice quiet and steady[6], so steady that he surprises himself.

"I think I should," answers Kesrit with a heavy tongue, "or at least bring you back to the camp and receive a great reward[7] from my khan."

"What if I tell him that you helped me escape, though? Then he'll have us both executed[8]," says Timucin.

"Yes, perhaps," says Kesrit after thinking these words over with obvious difficulty, "so it's best I kill you now and bring back nothing more than your head."

"Quite possibly," says Timucin, still astonished by the relaxed tone of his voice. Yet he really is not afraid, despite the fact that he is chained and that Kesrit is standing in front of him with his sword drawn[9] – and that the Tajin has decided to kill him.

Kesrit looks slightly confused, but then nods and lifts his sword a little higher. Timucin, filled with the confidence[10] of the dragon, continues talking as if he were chatting away to a friend[11].

1 **slightly slurred** – *leicht lallend*
2 **to follow the call of nature** – *dem Ruf der Natur folgen*
3 **to get lost** – *sich verlaufen*
4 **the slow slur of his speech** – *seine schleppende Art zu sprechen*
5 **to exchange pleasantries** – *Höflichkeiten austauschen*
6 **steady** – *fest*
7 **reward** – *Belohnung*
8 **to execute** – *hinrichten*
9 **with his sword drawn** – *mit gezogenem Schwert*
10 **confidence** – *Gelassenheit, Selbstbewusstsein*
11 **as if he were chatting away with a friend** – *im Plauderton*

"Perhaps, however, you should have a look in your yurt first, and check all of your saddles and bridles[1] and everything else you own." Kesrit's eyes are narrow, but they get even narrower.

"What is the point of all of this, Khan of the Pigs?"

"Well, perhaps your khan will not only be missing[2] a prisoner, but also his most valuable bit of booty[3]. That chain of pure gold that he looted[4] two years ago, you know the one." He shrugs his shoulders: "Now, wouldn't it be unpleasant if it were to be found in your tent of all places[5]?"

The drunkenness in Kesrit's eyes is immediately replaced with fear.

"You're lying!" he hisses[6].

"Am I?" answers Timucin quietly. It is the power of the dragon, Sarantuya's strength which, he now realises, has been in him all along[7]. That is how he has been able to hold on[8] for so long.

Now don't forget, little Genghis, I am you. Have you forgotten that already?

"Well, maybe I should kill you and then check my tent before I go to the khan and throw your head at his feet," considers Kesrit.

"Yes, as long as you are good at finding things. I would not be so sure, though: I've had the nail I used to open the lock for two years and you haven't noticed."

Kesrit is silent. He doesn't let his sword drop, but grinds his teeth audibly[9] and steps towards Timucin, almost without noticing it himself.

Just another step, not even that.

"You're a clever little lad, Khan of the Pigs," says the warrior after a while, "but it's not always a good thing to be clever, you know?"

1 **bridle** – *Zügel*
2 **to be missing sth.** – *etw. vermissen*
3 **booty** – *Beute*
4 **to loot sth.** – *sich erbeuten*
5 **of all places** – *ausgerechnet*
6 **to hiss** – *zischen*
7 **all along** – *die ganze Zeit*
8 **to hold on** – *durchhalten*
9 **audibly** – *hörbar*

"That is your choice," answers Timucin, his voice contemptuous[1] like that of the dragon, "for I have nothing more to lose. If you kill me now, I shall be as dead as I shall be if you take me back and your khan kills me: and my name is not Khan of the Pigs. I am Genghis!"

"What do you think I'm going to do?" asks Kesrit, angry but also slightly unsettled[2].

"Let me go," answers Timucin, "and loosen up my yoke a little so that I can go faster. If they catch me, then I shall say you helped me escape – and that will be the end of you[3], too."

"Nobody will believe you," says Kesrit, but he does not seem to quite believe his own words.

"Or we could flee[4] together," continues Timucin in the same tone as before, "because we would have a better chance together. I still have friends who would help us – me and you."

The last sentence is a complete lie, but Kesrit thinks about it for a moment, a long moment, before lifting his sword even higher and shaking his head:

"I'll take the risk!"

Timucin will not, of course, and as the warrior lifts his sword higher ready to swing, Timucin leaps at him[5] and pulls his body down to the left. Yet drunk or not, Kesrit is still twice as strong as Timucin, and reacts quickly. Just the soft brush of the yoke against his chin is enough to make him shout loudly, but he falls backwards and, before he can start to fight back through his drunkenness, Timucin rams the yoke so hard into his temples[6] that he loses consciousness.

1 **contemptuous** – *verächtlich*
2 **unsettled** – *verunsichert*
3 **that will be the end of you** – *dann ist es um dich geschehen*
4 **to flee** – *fliehen*
5 **to leap at sb.** – *jdn. anspringen*
6 **temple** – *Schläfe*

The Fight

TR. 12

Timucin has barely gone a few steps into the night when his conscience almost forces him to go back. He almost does, wants to make sure that the tattooed warrior is still alive. Perhaps it is the memory of all the little cruelties Kesrit has done to him, however, that keeps him from doing so. Kesrit has done a lot to him, certainly, but he doesn't deserve a shattered chin.

For a while, he moves along the river; then he heads east. The terrain is soon so rough that he can barely keep going and, despite the fact that he has spent five years here, he has only been this way a few times, and only during the day. In the dark, with this yoke on his shoulders, it is getting more and more difficult to keep moving. He soon stops counting how often he falls.

He tries to comfort himself with the thought that it will be almost impossible to follow him on horseback. But perhaps that will not be necessary, since there is a good chance that he will break his neck. Once or twice, however, the yoke breaks his falls and stops him injuring himself badly. The blood stuck to it is no longer just Kesrit's but his own, too. Meanwhile, he is getting weak faster than he expected. He's not even sure if he will make it to the dawn[1].

Is that what I have taught you, little Genghis? To discourage[2] yourself?

"You taught me to be alone," answers Timucin, "and I've quite enough experience of that, thank you very much."

The time was needed, little Genghis, replies the dragon.

"What for? So that I know what it means to be lonely?" hisses Timucin.

That is the price that all great men have to pay, in one way or another. Why did you not kill Kesrit?

Timucin does not understand what being alone has to do with killing Kesrit, and so does not answer at all for the sake of caution[3]. Instead, he

1 **dawn** – *Sonnenaufgang*
2 **to discourage sb.** – *jdn. entmutigen*
3 **for the sake of caution** – *vorsichtshalber*

spends a few moments making sure that he finds his way in the almost complete darkness. In front of him there is something huge, something slightly darker than the black night sky. There are no stars, which is why he can see it.

Someday, you will have to decide whether others live or die, thrive[1] *or starve*[2]*, little Genghis. Perhaps you will even spare*[3] *an entire people, because you know what it means to be tortured.*

"You mean that you let them take me prisoner so that I know what it is like to be one and therefore do not take any prisoners myself?"

With your complicated way of explaining perfectly simple things, you should become a diplomat, jokes Sarantuya, *but yes, you are right. You did not kill him* precisely because *you hate him and he made your life hell for five years.*

"Yes, that sounds logical."

It is, insists the dragon inside him, *because if you had killed him, you would be exactly like him. And in spite of everything, there is a part of you that is afraid of that.*

It takes a few moments for him to understand what he has just heard.

"Despite everything?" he murmurs: "Still?"

Sarantuya does not just refuse[4] to answer these words, but does not react at all. She speaks as if he had not spoken them. *Perhaps the day will come when you have to decide about the fate of an entire people, little Genghis,* she says instead. *Perhaps your decisions will be different if you know what pain and suffering*[5] *just a word or a gesture may mean for many, many people.*

Whilst he is still thinking about these words, he gets slower and slower. He has trouble staying on his legs. The shadow that has darkened the stars has become even larger and, while it promises to make things difficult for his pursuers, it will also be very difficult for him to climb.

1 **to thrive** – *gedeihen*
2 **to starve** – *hungern*
3 **to spare** – *verschonen*
4 **to refuse to do sth.** – *sich weigern, etw. zu tun*
5 **pain and suffering** – *Leid*

He approaches the obstacle[1], slower than ever before and now stopping to catch his breath[2]. Eventually, he finds himself in front of a solid, flat wall of rock, towering[3] over him, at least one and a half or perhaps even two times the height of a fully-grown man – not that this makes much of a difference to him in his yoke, his arms uselessly trapped inside it too. It might just as well be ten times as high as a man; it might just as well go up to the heavens.

Timucin slowly begins to understand why his guard was so unconcerned[4]: what is the point of running away when there is nowhere to run away to?

This line of thought does not discourage him, however, but makes him more determined[5]. Although he knows how pointless[6] it is, he takes a few steps along the cliff face and then turns back on his own track until he finds a rock at chest height[7] with jagged[8] edges sharp like an axe blade[9], sharp enough for the job. Gently, he sinks to his knees, gathers his courage and tries to arm himself against[10] the pain that is bound to come.

Timucin throws the yoke against the rock with such a force that the hardened wood groans. It does not crack or break, however, and most of the force he has thrown into the rock reverberates back[11] on him. He gasps in pain, a strong pain behind his eyes that is trying hard to make him unconscious. Timucin clenches his teeth[12] and does not allow himself to shout. He throws the yoke at the rock once again, and again, until something grinds[13] horribly. He doesn't know whether it is the yoke or

1 **obstacle** – *Hindernis*
2 **to catch one's breath** – *Atem holen, schnaufen*
3 **to tower** – *emporstreben*
4 **unconcerned** – *sorglos*
5 **to make sb. more determined** – *jds. Trotz wecken*
6 **pointless** – *sinnlos*
7 **chest height** – *Brusthöhe*
8 **jagged** – *scharf, zerklüftet*
9 **axe blade** – *Axtklinge*
10 **to arm oneself against** – *sich gegen etw. bewaffnen*
11 **to reverberate back** – *zurückprallen*
12 **to clench one's teeth** – *die Zähne zusammenbeißen*
13 **to grind** – *knirschen*

his bones, and sinks to the ground, groaning with exhaustion[1]. Blood is running down his neck, his shoulders and his scratched wrists[2], and although the yoke is lying around him in pieces, he thinks he can still feel its weight. Just the thought of moving is more than he can bear.

Yet he must go on. In an hour at the latest, the sun will rise and the first of the Tajin will awake, hung over[3], but not too hung over to notice that their prisoner is gone.

There is something in front of him. Perhaps it just a shadow or the sound of his own blood in his ears, but it could be movements, sounds made by someone pursuing[4] him.

He cannot work out the difference, so he sits up, stumbles towards the cliffs and lifts his arms. All the muscles in his neck and upper arms hurt. The Tajin have not forced him to wear the yoke every moment of these last five years – after all, they didn't want to cripple[5] him – but they always forced him to wear it until he needed several hours to be able to move without being in pain. He is used to this now, however, and is sure that he will be able to bear the pain and force his muscles to climb.

DRACHENFRAGE

How does Timucin escape the yoke?

What he has trouble bearing, however, is the brutal punch that hits him between the shoulder blades and throws him so hard against the rocks that he is, once again, almost unconscious.

"Do you know what? I've considered it, Khan of the Pigs," says a voice behind him in the darkness, "and I think I'll take the risk and throw your head at the feet of my khan. Then I'll tell him the same story you just tried to blackmail[6] me with."

1 **exhaustion** – *Erschöpfung*
2 **wrist** – *Handgelenk*
3 **hung over** – *verkatert*
4 **to pursue sb.** – *jdn. verfolgen, jagen*
5 **to cripple sb.** – *jdn. verkrüppeln*
6 **to blackmail sb.** – *jdn. erpressen*

Why does Sarantuya not help him? Where is the power of the dragon when he needs it?

Kesrit pulls him back to his feet and punches him again. He flies against the rock and hits the back of his head. He can taste his own blood, but at least he can see the stars now – coloured stars in front of his eyes.

"I will just tell our khan the same story you just told me," says Kesrit again, "and he will believe me. After all, he knows what a bunch of scoundrels and cheats[1] your clan are." He shakes his head regretfully[2].

"I know I should have never have gone along with your plan. But it is still not too late to correct this mistake[3]."

He lifts his sword – and something speeds down from the skies, invisible and powerful, something that throws Kesrit into the darkness with such a force that he does not even have time to shout in surprise[4]. Only a few seconds later, Timucin hears him fall against a cliff somewhere.

1 **scoundrels and cheats** – *Schwindler und Schlitzohren*
2 **regretfully** – *mit Bedauern*
3 **to correct a mistake** – *einen Fehler wiedergutmachen*
4 **... that he does not even have time to shout in surprise** – *...dass ihm nicht einmal mehr Zeit für einen überraschten Schrei bleibt*

A Friend

TR. 13

Sarantuya, he thinks, exhausted. The dragon has come at last to stand with him[1], although clearly not to give him strength. He sinks back to his knees and must now summon up[2] every last drop of willpower[3] to resist the tempting call of unconsciousness[4]. Shadows are dancing around him in rings, he hears strange noises, and thinks he can feel the touch of an extremely soft yet strong hand. His back presses against rocks that are still warm, water splashes[5] onto his face, water that is so cold that it feels like needles stabbing him.

Timucin groans as he opens his eyes and, for a moment, sees nothing but darkness. After he has blinked once or twice, however, this darkness takes on form and turns into a face. Timucin's heart stops beating[6] for a moment and he is not sure whether he has just lost consciousness and had a particularly bad nightmare – or worse.

Perhaps this is the opposite of a nightmare, my little Genghis. Were not five years enough to teach you patience?

Timucin blinks, and the darkness above him slowly turns into a familiar face, a face he has not expected to see at this place and at this time.

"You?" he murmurs.

As Timucin looks at him in the pale starlight, he realises that Chuzir has aged more than five years. There is a scar on his cheek that is not fully healed and a darkness in his eyes that Timucin cannot – and does not want to – know the meaning of.

"Chuzir?" he says after a while, because his brother in oath does not answer and looks away from him. How did he get here – and what is he doing here?

1 **to stand with sb.** – *jdm. beistehen*
2 **to summon up** – *aufbringen, zusammennehmen*
3 **willpower** – *Willenskraft*
4 **unconsciousness** – *Bewusstlosigkeit*
5 **splash** – *spritzen*
6 **his heart stops beating** – *sein Herz setzt aus*

Chuzir puts water to Timucin's lips. He has just sprayed him with it to stop him from becoming unconscious.

"Chuzir?" asks Timucin the third time after he has drunk a few deep gulps of water. Chuzir reties the pouch and continues to avoid Timucin's eyes.

"Do not call me that, my Khan, for I am not worthy[1] of being spoken to by name." Timucin thinks this is stupid. It is like his throat is sewn together and he cannot answer.

"Let me see your wounds[2], my Khan," asks Chuzir.

Timucin has not realised that he is wounded[3]. Injuries[4] and pain have been a part of his life since he became the "Khan of the Pigs" amongst the Tajin. Yet he has to clench his teeth as Chuzir sees to his wounds on his wrists and neck with water, healing[5] balm and bandages[6] – and no small amount of force. Yet once Chuzir has finished, most of the pain he caused himself breaking the yoke has gone. He nods and tries to show his gratitude[7].

"Thanks."

Chuzir starts at[8] this word as if were a harsh reproach.

"Later I shall find someone who has a better understanding of such matters[9] to take care of your wounds, my Khan. I cannot do it at the moment."

"Of course," answers Timucin, "you are a warrior: you are better at making wounds than at nursing[10] them, right?" Somehow he manages not only to put on a silly grin, but also to punch Chuzir playfully in the

1 **to not be worthy of sth.** – *etw. nicht wert sein*
2 **wound** – *Wunde*
3 **wounded** – *verletzt*
4 **injury** – *Verletzung*
5 **healing balm** – *heilende Salbe*
6 **bandage** – *Verband*
7 **gratitude** – *Dankbarkeit*
8 **to start at sth.** – *wegen etw. zusammenfahren*
9 **who has a better understanding of such matters** – *der sich besser darauf versteht*
10 **to nurse sb.'s wounds** – *jds. Wunden verarzten*

ribs, even if this does cause him more pain than it does Chuzir. Chuzir himself looks nervous and does not know where to look[1].

"In an hour the sun will rise, my Khan," he says nervously, "and it will not take them long to find your tracks. Can you walk?"

Timucin does not know whether he can or not, but he puts out his hand and lets Chuzir help him to his feet.

He is able to stand up, but after taking a couple of steps, he falls over. Chuzir holds him and stops him from falling. For a while, his brother in oath pretends[2] that this is completely normal and even makes a few lame[3] jokes, but after a while he gives up and lets Timucin sink to the ground with a pitiful[4] shrug of his shoulders.

"There's no point," he says. "Wait here: I'll go and get the others."

"What others?" asks Timucin, alarmed.

"My father and I were not the only ones who did not agree with what Tedschen and his people made of our clan," answers Chuzir in a very serious tone: "He is nothing but a coward who crawls[5] on the floor when he is confronted with someone stronger[6], but is all the crueller to his own people. We do not need a khan of that nature."

He goes before Timucin can answer. Lying there, Timucin feels an incredible sense of loneliness, lost as if this desolate[7] cliff were the whole world, and he the only person left on it.

Why don't you help me? he thinks to the dragon. *You promised to never leave me alone.*

And what do you want me to do now, little Genghis? Sarantuya's voice sounds scornful. *Do you want me to teach you to fly and to spit fire*[8] *so that you can burn your enemies? You know that it does not work that way.*

So you are just a powerless voice, then? asks Timucin angrily.

1 **he does not know where to look** – *er weiß nicht wohin mit seinem Blick*
2 **to pretend that** – *so tun, als ob*
3 **lame** – *lahm*
4 **pitiful** – *bedauernd*
5 **to crawl** – *kriechen*
6 **when he is confronted with someone stronger** – *wenn er einem Stärkeren gegenübersteht*
7 **desolate** – *öde*
8 **to spit fire** – *Feuer speien*

In a way, yes, admits the dragon, *but in another... no.*
So what are you good for, then? asks Timucin bitterly.
Perhaps for you to finally learn to listen to yourself, little Khan, says Sarantuya. As she continues to speak, Timucin hears more than just her silent voice. He hears an echo, too, from a time long ago, a whisper of an age of legends and myths. These are inaudible sounds from a time when there were dragons and giants and fabulous beings, a time when humans had not even been thought of[1].
I am the last of my kind, little Genghis.
The last dragon? says Timucin, frightened.
The last one who believes in the world of humans.
The last one who believes in us*?* repeats Timucin, confused. He wants to laugh, but he cannot. *Aren't you getting a little confused there? It is supposed to be* humans *who believe in dragons, not the other way round!*
And how do you know that it isn't quite the opposite? asks Sarantuya. *Perhaps you are all just a part of my dream.*
What dream is that?
Perhaps the dream of things going back to the way they were. There was a time when many of us had a friend from your world, and it was a time in which many of your kind commanded the power of a dragon[2]. Yet too many of you misused this power, and so more and more of us turned our backs on you[3]. Now there is only me – and you. The others believe that the time of humans and dragons together is past, but I believe differently. I believe in you, little Genghis.
Why? asks Timucin, confused.
This time, however, there is no answer from the dragon. Instead, he hears sounds and sees a shadow coming towards him. Although he is sure that it can only be Chuzir, his heart begins to beat faster.
It is Chuzir. His brother in oath is fast, but silent and elegant in a way that makes Timucin slightly jealous. Not only does he see how much

1 **when humans had not even been thought of** – *als man an Menschen noch nicht einmal dachte; als der Mensch noch nicht einmal eine Idee war*
2 **to command sb.'s power** – *über jds. Macht gebieten*
3 **to turn one's back on sb.** – *sich von jdm. abwenden*

older and more experienced Chuzir has become, but also the kind of life he has been living for the past five years. It is a life that has probably not been any less full of privations, hardship and pain than his own ordeal[1] at the hands of the Tajin, but he has had all the things Timucin has not. It is almost as if Chuzir has read his thoughts and, as he approaches, drops to one knee and sinks his head in deference[2]: "My Khan."

"What is this nonsense?" murmurs Timucin.

"The others are here," says Chuzir, not really answering the question. "We must hurry, my Khan."

"What is all this? Who are the others?" asks Timucin again. Chuzir does not answer his question, but stands up after another moment. Despite having said they must hurry, he does not make any sign[3] of turning or moving.

"There is something else," he says hesitantly[4] and still avoiding Timucin's eyes. It takes a little more time before he reaches behind him and pulls a single arrow out of the quiver on his back. Fresh blood shines on the metal arrowhead[5] in the dark. There is even blood on the shaft[6] and on one of the three shining white[7] feathers. Despite the fact that he has not seen this arrow for five years, he recognises it instantly – how could he forget it?

"Our arrow of friendship," says Timucin, remembering how long, long ago they exchanged arrows of friendship – back in the good old days when his father was still khan and when everything happened as it should[8]. The exchange of the arrows was supposed to seal[9] their friendship, but everything happened differently in the end.

"You still have the arrow after all this time?" asks Timucin.

1 **ordeal** – *Martyrium*
2 **in deference** – *demütig, respektvoll*
3 **to not make any sign of doing sth.** – *keine Anstalten machen, etwas zu tun*
4 **hesitantly** – *zögernd*
5 **arrowhead** – *Pfeilspitze*
6 **shaft** – *Schaft*
7 **shining white** – *strahlend weiß*
8 **to happen as it should** – *seinen geregelten Gang gehen*
9 **to seal** – *besiegeln*

Chuzir is silent. You can see him struggling to think of what to say. He stretches out his hand as if to return the arrow to Timucin, and then withdraws his arm again.

"Whose blood is that?" asks Timucin.

"Kesrit's," answers Chuzir. "I had no choice. He would have beaten you to death otherwise[1].

"I know," says Timucin, taking back the arrow from Chuzir after some time. As he does, he thinks about something.

"How did you know his name?" he asks Chuzir

"I told you I had somebody there looking after you," says Chuzir, "and I paid him well, even if I probably should have slit his throat instead."

"Kesrit?" asks Timucin in genuine surprise: "You mean the man who made me the 'Khan of the Pigs' and tortured me every day for five years?"

"I told him to do that," says Chuzir, "because it would have been difficult for him to carry out his job if he had been too gentle with you." Before Timucin can reply, Chuzir stops him speaking with a wave of his hand, and then takes the arrow out of his hand. With a hard crack, he breaks it into two unequal halves. It is a sharp sound, and Timucin is afraid that it will travel all the way to the Tajin camp.

"What... why?" gasps Timucin, looking horrified at the broken arrow.

As quietly as he has just taken and broken the arrow, Chuzir hands him back the two pieces before reaching below his belt with the other hand and drawing a dagger. He offers the hilt[2] to Timucin before dropping to his knees a second time and sinking his head, making a show of[3] offering Timucin his unprotected[4] neck.

"Kill me, my Khan," he says, "for I have betrayed you and brought shame to myself and my family. I do not deserve to live any longer."

If he had not felt the seriousness of these words, Timucin would probably have laughed out loud at them. Since he sees that Chuzir is serious, however, he can only stare at him in disbelief.

1 **he would have beaten you to death otherwise** – *sonst hätte er dich erschlagen*
2 **hilt** – *Heft, Griff (eines Schwerts)*
3 **to make a show of doing sth.** – *etw. demonstrativ machen*
4 **unprotected** – *ungeschützt*

"What do you mean by this?" Timucin asks. "Betrayed me? I might be wrong[1], but I get the impression[2] that you just saved my life!"

Chuzir shakes his head strongly.

"If it weren't for me, you would not have been taken prisoner in the first place," he insists, "and Arbesa and your mother would still be free, too. I have betrayed our friendship and therefore I break the arrow and release you from the oath which I myself have already broken. If the Khan wishes me to pay for this with my life, then I shall."

Timucin sighs, long and deep.

"If I ever come across[3] 'the Khan', then I will ask him," promises Timucin facetiously[4], "yet for the moment, I have only one question. Please answer me in all honesty."

Chuzir does not reply, but nods silently. Timucin picks up the two pieces of the broken arrow.

"Did you really believe in the power of the arrow back then?"

Chuzir nods. He looks confused and slightly afraid.

"Then your Khan has an order that you must obey[5]," continues Timucin: "You must find a long, straight branch[6] and make me a new arrow to seal our friendship again."

DRACHENFRAGE

Why does Chuzir break the arrow of friendship?

For a moment, their eyes meet. It is as if the two boys who made their oath of friendship all those years ago are now looking at each other again, not knowing how tricky the path ahead will be.

Suddenly, the chinking and rattling[7] of metal can be heard. Quiet voices are getting louder as they approach. Chuzir jumps up.

1 **I might be wrong, but... (Redewendung)** – *ich kann mich ja täuschen, aber...*
2 **I get the impression** – *mir kommt es so vor*
3 **to come across sb.** – *jdm. begegnen*
4 **facetiously** – *witzelnd, spöttisch*
5 **to obey an order** – *einem Befehl gehorchen*
6 **branch** – *Ast*
7 **chinking and rattling** – *Klimpern und Klirren*

"There they are! Do not be afraid: they are my people!"

Timucin, who has just bolted up[1], relaxes again and tries to pierce[2] the darkness with his eyes. At first, he sees nothing but ghostly outlines in the dawn twilight[3]. Slowly, he recognises half a dozen armoured[4] warriors coming over the rocks. The help he has needed for so long is now here!

His time as the Khan of the Pigs has ended and his brother in oath is at his side. Now Timucin will prove that he and no other is Khan of the Kijat – and he will see Arbesa again, whatever it takes[5].

1 **to bolt up** – *sich alarmiert aufrichten*
2 **to pierce** – *durchdringen*
3 **twilight** – *Zwielicht*
4 **armoured** – *in Rüstung*
5 **whatever it takes** – *koste es, was es wolle*

Fantasy-Vokabular

assault *Angriff*

armour *Rüstung, Harnisch*

attack *Angriff*

arrow *Pfeil*

dagger *Dolch*

to cast a spell on sb. *jmd. mit einem Zauber belegen, verzaubern*

to forge *schmieden*

to fight valiantly *sich tapfer schlagen*

rider *Ritter*

wisdom *Weisheit*

wise *weise*

legend *Mythos*

counsel *Rat*

magician *Magier*

combat *Kampf*

to draw a weapon *eine Waffe ziehen / spannen*

bow *Bogen*

quest for sth. *Suche / Streben nach etw.*

to curse oneself *sich verfluchen*

to swear an oath *einen Eid schwören*

brave *wacker*

darkness *Finsternis*

to be betrothed to sb. *jdm. versprochen sein*

creature *Wesen*

coward *Feigling*

defender *Verteidiger*

bandit *Räuber*

tribe *Stamm*

cowardly *feige*

sword *Schwert*

to quake *beben, zittern*

fellow *Gefährte*

to pillage *plündern*

feast *Gelage*

leader *Anführer*

battle *Schlacht*

noble *edel*

dragon *Drache*

sturdy steed *strammes Ross*

tower *Turm*

to banish sb. *jdn. verbannen, verjagen*

monstrous *ungeheuer*

to harry *verheeren, plündern*

to steal into sth. *sich in etw. hineinschleichen*

garment *Gewand*

to lay waste to sth. *etw. verwüsten*

potion *Zaubertrank*

secret *Geheimnis*

Englisch-deutsche Wortliste

abyss	*Abgrund*
admit	*gestehen*
advance	*vorankommen, sich vorwärts bewegen*
against all odds	*entgegen aller Wahrscheinlichkeit*
agonised	*gequält*
aiming behind him	*hinter sich zielend*
all along	*die ganze Zeit*
all the blood has drained out of her fingers	*alles Blut ist aus ihren Fingern gewichen*
all too well	*nur zu gut*
ally	*Verbündeter*
alright	*schon recht; ganz richtig*
ambigious	*mehrdeutig*
And that's the end of the matter! (Redewendung)	*Und Schluss!*
appallingly	*entsetzlich, furchtbar*
appear	*auftauchen*
appropriate	*angemessen*
approving	*beifällig*
arduous	*anstrengt, mühsam*
argument	*Streit, Auseinandersetzung*
arm oneself against	*sich gegen etw. bewaffnen*
arm oneself for war	*zum Krieg rüsten*
armour	*Rüstung*
armoured	*in Rüstung*
armoured scales	*Panzerschuppen*
arrow	*Pfeil*
arrowhead	*Pfeilspitze*
as if he were chatting away with a friend	*im Plauderton*
as if it has been struck by lighting	*wie vom Blitz getroffen*
as if to mock him	*wie um ihn zu verspotten*
as is their way	*wie es ihre Art ist*
ascent	*Anstieg, Auffahrt*
aside	*Nebenbemerkung*
astonishing	*unglaublich, atemberaubend, erstaunlich*
astonishment	*Erstaunen*
audibly	*hörbar*
authority	*Souveränität*
avoid sb.'s gaze	*jdn.s Blick ausweichen*
awesome	*Ehrfucht gebietend*
axe blade	*Axtklinge*
bandage	*Verband*
banish a thought	*einen Gedanken verscheuchen*
bare	*bloß, unbedeckt, unbekleidet; auch: blattlos*
bare blade	*blanke Klinge*
be astonished	*staunen*
be at fault	*schuld sein*
be fast asleep	*fest schlafen*
be headed for sth.	*zu einem Ort unterwegs sein*
be missing sth.	*etw. vermissen*
be mistaken	*sich täuschen, sich irren*
be on sb.'s heels	*jdm. auf den Fersen sein*

be stuck	*feststecken*
be tempted	*verführt werden*
Be that as it may.	*Sei's drum.*
be used to sth.	*etw. gewohnt sein*
be violently sick	*sich qualvoll erbrechen*
bear	*ertragen*
bearable	*erträglich*
become aware of sth.	*etw. gewahren*
beg	*betteln*
beguiling	*betörend*
being	*Wesen*
belongings	*Habe*
bend double	*sich krümmen*
bend down	*sich bücken*
betray	*verraten*
betrayal	*Betrug*
betrothed (altertümlich)	*Verlobte(r)*
blackmail sb.	*jdn. erpressen*
blackness	*Schwärze*
blade	*Schwert, Klinge*
blink	*blinzeln*
blink sth. away	*etw. wegblinzeln*
bloody	*blutig*
blurred	*verschwommen*
bolt up	*sich alarmiert aufrichten*
bonds	*Fessel*
booty	*Beute*
bottomless	*unergründlich*
boulder	*Geröll*
bound to his word	*an sein Wort gebunden*
bow	*senken*
branch	*Ast*
breathtaking	*atemberaubend*
bribe sb.	*jdn. bestechen*
bridle	*Zügel*
brood over sth	*über etw. brüten, nachdenken*
brother in oath	*Schwurbruder*
bucket	*Eimer*
by force	*mit Gewalt*
by your hand	*von deiner Hand*
cackling	*Gegacker*
captivity	*Gefangenschaft*
captor	*Fänger*
cart	*Karre*
casually	*wie unabsichtlich, beiläufig, zufällig*
catch one's breat	*Atem holen, schnaufen*
catch oneself wondering if…	*sich beim Gedanken ertappen, ob…*
catch up	*aufholen*
ceaselessly	*ohne Unterbrechung*
celebratory	*feierlich*
ceremonial	*feierlich*
chained	*gefesselt*
challenge sb.	*jdn. fordern*
charade	*Affentheater*
cheek	*Wange*
chest height	*Brusthöhe*
chilling	*schneidend, eisig*
chinking and rattling	*Klimpern und Klirren*
chunk	*Brocken*
claim that	*etw. behaupten*
clash	*sich überschlagen*
Clear off!	*Hau ab!*
clench one's fist	*die Hand zur Faust ballen*
clench one's teeth	*die Zähne zusammenbeißen*
cliff	*Fels*

clink	*klirren*
collapse	*zusammenbrechen*
combat	*Kampf*
come across sb.	*jdm. begegnen*
comfort	*Trost, Annehmlichkeit*
comfort	*trösten*
comforting	*beruhigend*
command sb.' s power	*über jds. Macht gebieten*
commandment	*Gebot*
commit	*begehen*
confidence	*Gelassenheit, Selbstbewusstsein*
confidently	*überzeugt, selbstbewusst*
consciousness	*Bewusstsein*
consist of sth.	*aus etw. bestehen*
consistently	*beharrlich*
contain	*beinhalten*
contempt	*Verachtung*
contemptuous	*verächtlich*
contradict sb.	*jdm. widersprechen*
conviction	*Überzeugung*
correct a mistake	*einen Fehler wiedergutmachen*
counsel	*Rat*
counter	*widersprechen*
countless	*zahllos*
cover one's tracks	*die Spuren verwischen*
covered in scratches	*zerschunden*
coward	*Feigling*
crawl	*kriechen*
creep	*kriechen*
creep in	*hineinschleichen*
creep up on sb.	*sich an jdn. heranschleichen*
crime	*Frevel*
cripple sb.	*jdn. verkrüppeln*
crouch	*sich ducken*
crouch down	*in die Hocke gehen*
crucial	*sehr wichtig*
cruel	*grausam*
cruelty	*Graumsamkeit*
cry sb.	*sich bei jdm. ausweinen*
curious	*neugierig*
curse	*fluchen*
curt	*schroff, spröde*
curtly	*schnippisch*
cymbal	*Zimbel*
dagger	*Dolch*
dare to do sth.	*es wagen, etw. zu tun*
daring	*tollkühn*
darken	*verdunkeln*
dawn	*Morgendämmerung, Sonnenaufgang*
decide how sth. is meant	*etw. deuten*
decipher	*entziffern*
declare oneself sth.	*sich selbst zu etw. ausrufen*
deep down	*tief im Innersten*
deepen	*vertiefen*
degradation	*Entwürdigung, Demütigung*
degrade sb.	*erniedrigen*
deliberately	*bewusst*
delicate	*zart*
delirious	*phantasierend*
deny a truth	*die Wahrheit leugnen*
derogatory	*abfällig*
descent	*Abstieg*
desolate	*öde*
destroy	*zerstören*

dew	*Tau*
die in agony	*elendig sterben, unter Qualen sterben*
dig	*graben*
direst need	*höchste Not*
disastrous circumstances	*desaströse Umstände*
disbelief	*Unglauben*
disbelievingly	*ungläubig*
discourage sb.	*jdn. entmutigen*
dishonourable	*ehrlos*
dispirited	*mutlos*
dispute	*Streit*
distrustful	*misstrauisch*
disturbing	*verstörend*
disturbing	*verstörend*
do not make any sign of doing sth.	*keine Anstalten machen, etw. zu tun*
do sb. the favour of doing sth.	*jdm. einen Gefallen tun*
drag oneself along	*sich dahinschleppen*
draught	*Zug*
draw a sword from a scabbard	*ein Schwert aus der Scheide ziehen*
dread sth.	*sich vor etw. fürchten*
drink oneself in unconsciousness	*sich bis zur Bewusstlosigkeit betrinken*
emaciated	*abgemagert*
embers	*Glut*
embrace	*Umarmung*
emerge from sth.	*aus etw. auftauchen, aus etw. herauskommen*
encampment	*Lagerplatz*
endure	*ertragen*
enlightenment	*Erleuchtung*
erase one's traces	*seine Spuren verwischen*
escape	*entkommen*

escape sb.'s notice	*jdm. entgehen*
eternity	*Ewigkeit*
evenly formed	*gleichmäßig geformt*
eventually	*schließlich, endlich*
everyday	*alltäglich*
everything you were attached to	*alles, woran eure Herzen gehangen haben*
examine	*begutachten*
exchange pleasantries	*Höflichkeiten austauschen*
excuse	*Vorwand*
execute	*hinrichten*
exhausted	*erschöpft*
exhaustion	*Erschöpfung*
expansiveness	*Weite*
exquisite	*prachtvoll*
exterminate	*auslöschen*
eye sb.	*jdn. beäugen, jdn. anschauen*
facetiously	*witzelnd, spöttisch*
fade	*verblassen*
fashion	*Art, Weise; Mode*
fateful	*schicksalhaft*
feast	*Festmahl, Gelage*
fetch	*holen*
fiery	*feurig*
fight against sth.	*sich gegen etw. stellen*
fill somebody with fear	*jdm. Furcht einflößen*
flaky	*flockig*
flank	*Flanke*
flash	*Blitzen*
flash one's eyes at sb.	*jdn. anfunkeln*
flee	*fliehen*
fleeting	*flüchtig*
flight	*Flucht; Flug*

flock	*Herde*
fluffy	*flaumig*
flurry	*Gestöber*
foam	*Schaum*
follow the call of nature	*dem Ruf der Natur folgen*
for once and for all	*endgültig*
for some reason or another	*aus irgendeinem Grund*
for the sake of caution	*vorsichtshalber*
for which you may be thankful	*zu deinem Glück*
forbid	*verbieten*
foretaste	*Vorgeschmack*
forgive	*vergeben, verzeihen*
fragile	*zerbrechlich*
frown	*die Stirn runzeln*
full of privations	*reich an Entbehrungen*
fur coat	*Pelzmantel*
fur-lined	*pelzgefüttert*
gain on one's pursuers	*seinen Vorsprung ausbauen*
gap	*Spalt*
gasp	*keuchen*
Genghis Khan	*Dschingis Khan (der bekannte Khan der Mongolen, er lebte ca. 1155–1227)*
gentle	*sanftmütig*
gently	*sanft*
gesture sb. do sth.	*jdm. mit der Hand bedeuten, etw. zu tun*
get a move on	*sich sputen*
get inthe habit of doing sth.	*sich angewöhnen, etw. zu tun*
get lost	*sich verlaufen*
get one's bearings	*sich orientieren, sich einen Überblick verschaffen*
get out of here	*von hier zu entkommen*
get rid of sb.	*jdn. fortjagen, loswerden*
gift	*Geschenk*
giggle	*kichern*
give in sth.	*etw. zulassen*
give up	*aufgeben*
gleeful anticipation	*hämische Vorfreude*
glove	*Handschuh*
glower at sb.	*jdn. finster ansehen*
glowing	*glühend*
gods of fate	*Schicksalsgötter*
grant sb. a wish	*jdm. einen Wunsch erfüllen*
gratitude	*Dankbarkeit*
greedy	*gierig*
grief	*Trauer*
grimly determind	*grimmig entschlossen*
grind	*knirschen*
growl	*knurren*
guard	*hüten*
guard	*Wächter*
guilty	*schuldig*
gully	*Schlucht*
gulp	*Schluck*
gust of wind	*Windstoß*
haggard crone	*ausgezehrtes altes Weib*
half an hour's ride	*ein halbstündiger Ritt*
happen as it should	*seinen geregelten Gang gehen*
harassment	*Schikane*
harness	*Zaumzeug*

harry sb.	*jdn. ständig belästigen*
hasty	*übereilt, hastig*
have trouble doing sth.	*Mühe haben, etw. zu machen*
he does not know where to look	*er weiß nicht wohin mit seinem Blick*
he doesn't care if...	*es ist ihm gleich, ob...*
He feels the need to tell it.	*Es ist ihm ein Bedürfnis, es zu erzählen.*
he is disgusted by it	*es ist ihm tiefst zuwider*
He is taking his life into his hands.	*Dann geht es um sein Leben.*
He makes no secret of...	*Er macht kein Hehl aus...*
he might just as well...	*er könnte genauso gut...*
He would be long dead by now.	*Er wäre jetzt schon lange nicht mehr am Leben.*
He would give his eye teeth to do sth.	*Er würde seinen rechten Arm dafür geben, etw. zu tun*
He would have beaten you to death otherwise.	*Sonst hätte er dich erschlagen.*
healing balm	*heilende Salbe*
heap of rocks	*Haufen von Felsen*
hesitantly	*zögernd*
hesitate	*zögern*
hide	*Fell*
hiding place	*Versteck*
hilt	*Heft, Griff (eines Schwerts)*
his face falls	*er verliert die Kontrolle über seine Züge*
His heart stops beating	*sein Herz setzt aus*
his knee buckles slightly	*er geht ein Stück weit in die Knie*
his luck has run out	*sein Glückssträhne ist zu Ende*
hiss	*zischen*
hold on	*durchhalten*
hold sb. up	*jdn. aufhalten*
hollow	*Talkessel*
holy	*heilig*
honour	*Ehre*
hood	*Kapuze*
hoof	*Huf*
hopeless	*hoffnungslos, aussichtslos*
horrendous	*entsetzlich, grauenhaft*
horrifying	*grausam*
horror	*Entsetzen*
hostage	*Geißeln*
humiliate sb.	*jdn. demütigen*
humiliation	*Demütigung, Erniedrigung*
humility	*Demut*
humourous	*gutmütig, humorvoll*
hung over	*verkatert*
hunt	*jagen*
hurricane	*Wirbelsturm*
I get the impression	*Mir kommt es so vor*
I have no right to...	*es steht mir nicht zu,...*
I might be wrong, but... (Redewendung)	*Ich kann mich ja täuschen, aber...*
I should like nothing more than to...	*Nichts täte ich lieber, als...*
I was so angry with myself	*ich habe mir solche Vorwürfe gemacht*
I who...	*Ich, der ich...*

I would have put it a little more diplomatically.	*Ich hätte es ein wenig diplomatischer ausgedrückt.*
I would not have hesitated to die for you.	*Ich hätte nicht gezögert, für dich zu sterben.*
if it weren't for	*ohne*
If you will (altertümlich)	*Wenn du willst*
If you wish it of me…	*Wenn du es so willst, werde ich…*
Ilhan's face is full of hatred.	*Ilhans Gesicht verzerrt sich vor Hass.*
imaginary friend	*ausgedachter Freund*
impassable	*unpassierbar*
impenetrable	*undurchdringlich*
improvised	*improvisiert*
in a blink of an eye	*im Handumdrehen*
in a way	*irgendwie*
in chains	*gefesselt*
in deference	*demütig, respektvoll*
in one swift movement	*in einem Satz*
indulge in sth.	*sich in etw. ergehen*
inexperienced	*unerfahren*
injury	*Verletzung*
inscrutable	*undeutbar*
insist	*beharren*
intend to do sth.	*etw. vorhaben*
interrupt	*jdm. ins Wort fallen, unterbrechen*
invisible	*unsichtbares*
isolated	*fern, isoliert*
it can't be otherwise	*das bleibt nicht aus*
It does not matter one bit. (Redewendung)	*Es ist ganz egal.*
it is not fitting	*es ziemt sich nicht*
It is not the done thing for a Khan to kneel.	*Es ziemt sich nicht für einen Khan zu knien.*
It might just as well be. (Redewendung)	*Es läuft auf dasselbe hinaus.*
It would barely have been worth…	*Es hätte sich kaum gelohnt…*
itch	*jucken*
jab	*Stichelei; Schlag*
jab sb.	*jdn. boxen, jmd. einen (leichten) Stoß verpassen*
jagged	*scharf, zerklüftet*
jailor	*Kerkermeister*
jealous	*eifersüchtig*
jeer	*johlen*
jeering	*spöttisch*
jibe sb.	*jmd. foppen*
jingle	*klimpern*
joy	*Freude*
jump	*erschrocken zusammenfahren*
just this moment	*ausgerechnet jetzt*
jut out	*aus etw. ragen*
keep an eye on sb.	*jdn. im Auge behalten*
keep an eye out for sb.	*nach jmd. Ausschau halten*
keep control of one's feelings	*seine Gefühle mäßigen*
keep one's balance	*das Gleichgewicht nicht verlieren*
keep one's end of the bargain	*ehrenhaft sein, seine Versprechen einhalten*
keep sb. going	*jmd. Kraft geben*
kindred (altertümlich)	*Familie, Seinesgleichen*
lad	*Junge*

lame	*lahm*
lame	*lahmen*
lead	*Vorsprung*
leafless	*blattlos*
leap	*springen*
leap at sb.	*jdn. anspringen*
leave it at sth.	*es bei etw. belassen*
leave the dirty work to others	*anderen das schmutzige Tun überlassen*
lessen	*zurückgehen*
let alone	*geschweige denn*
lighten	*aufhellen*
limb	*Glied*
limp	*humpeln*
literally	*buchstäblich*
little more than what we had on our backs	*wenig mehr als dem, was wir auf dem Leib hatten*
lock	*Schloss*
loneliness	*Einsamkeit*
look down at sb.	*auf jdn. herabsehen*
look out for sb.	*auf jdn. Acht geben*
loot sth.	*sich erbeuten*
lunge at sb.	*sich auf jdn. stürzen*
magnificent	*prachtvoll*
make a show of doing sth.	*etw. demonstrativ machen*
make for sth. (altertümlich)	*sich auf den Weg machen nach*
make haste (altertümlich)	*sich sputen*
make no bones of the fact that...	*keinen Zweifel daran lassen, dass...*
make out	*erkennen*
make progress	*vorankommen*
make sb. more determined	*jds. Trotz wecken*
make sth. of sb.	*jdn. einschätzen*
make sure	*sich vergewissern*
makeshift	*provisorisch*
malice	*Bosheit*
malicious	*hämisch, schadenfroh*
man of his word	*Ehrenmann*
manhood	*Mannesalter*
manoeuvre	*bugsieren*
mare's milk	*Stutenmilch*
marshy	*morastig*
meaningless	*bedeutungslos, sinnlos*
mercy	*Gnade*
might	*Kraft*
misuse	*missbrauchen*
mockingly	*spöttisch*
moist	*feucht*
more dangerous than most would assume	*gefährlicher als man gemeinhin annimmt*
mouthful	*(kräftiger) Schluck*
move against sb.	*gegen jdn. ziehen*
muddy	*schlammig*
mumble	*murmeln*
murmur	*murmeln*
muscular	*muskulös*
muster	*aufbringen, zusammennehmen*
nail	*Nagel*
naive	*naiv*
nastiness	*Bosheit*
neigh	*Wiehern*
nimble	*geschickt, wendig*
nostrils	*Nüstern*
Not after what he has done to her.	*Nicht nach dem, was er ihr angetan hatte.*
not at all reproachful	*frei von jedem Vorwurf*

not be worthy of sth.	*etw. nicht wert sein*
not without cause	*nicht zu Unrecht*
nurse sb.'s wounds	*jds. Wunden verarzten*
oath	*Eid*
obey an order	*einem Befehl gehorchen*
object	*aufbegehren*
obstacle	*Hindernis*
odd	*komisch*
of all places	*ausgerechnet*
on the run	*auf der Flucht*
opposite	*entgegengesetzt*
oracling	*Orakeln*
ordeal	*Martyrium*
outline	*Umriss*
overwhelming	*gewaltig, überwältigend*
ox	*Ochse*
packhorse	*Packpferd*
pain and suffering	*Leid*
pale	*blass*
pasture	*Weide*
pathetic	*jämmerlich*
patience	*Geduld*
peak	*Gifpel*
pen	*Pferch*
penmate	*Mitbewohner im Pferch*
pennant	*Wimpel*
petty	*kleinlich*
pierce	*durchdringen*
pinch oneself	*sich kneifen*
pious	*fromm*
pitiful	*bedauernd*
play a joke on sb.	*einen Scherz mit jmd. treiben*
plea	*Bitte*
plead with sb. for sth.	*jdn. um etw. anflehen*
pleasure	*Vergnügen*
plenty	*genug, reichlich*
plod	*trotten, sich dahinschleppen, sich abmühen*
pointedly	*betont*
pointless	*sinnlos*
poisoned	*vergiftet*
poke fun at sb.	*jdn. verspotten*
polish	*polieren*
pool	*Suhle*
possession	*Habseligkeit*
post	*Pfosten*
potion	*Trunk, Gebräu*
pouch	*Beutel*
Praise Tenghis!	*Tenghis sei dank!*
precious	*kostbar*
precious treasure	*wertvoller Schatz*
presence	*Gegenwart*
preserve	*haltbar machen*
pretend that	*so tun, als ob*
prey	*Beute*
promise	*Versprechen*
properly	*wirklich, zünftig, recht*
pull a face	*die Miene verziehen*
pull sb.'s leg	*jmd. auf den Arm nehmen*
pulverise	*zerschmettern*
punch	*Faustschlag*
purse	*Geldbeutel*
pursue sb.	*jdn. verfolgen, jagen*
pursuer	*Verfolger*
put sb./sth. out of its misery	*jdn.s Leiden ein Ende setzen*

quicksand	*Treibsand*
quip	*spöttisch/witzelnd antworten,*
quirky	*schief*
quiver	*Köcher*
quizzically	*fragend*
rage	*Wut*
rampant	*zugewuchert, verfilzt*
ransom	*Lösegeld*
ravine	*Hohlweg*
refuse help	*Hilfe ablehnen*
refuse to do sth.	*sich weigern, etw. zu tun*
regretfully	*mit Bedauern*
reins	*Zügel*
relieve sb. of sth.	*jdn. von etw. erlösen*
relieved	*erleichtert*
reluctant	*unwillig*
remain loyal sb.	*jdm. die Treue halten*
remove	*zurücknehmen, entnehmen*
reproach	*Zurechtweisung, Vorwurf*
reproach sb.	*jdm. Vorwürfe machen*
reproachfully	*vorwurfsvoll*
resist sb.	*sich jdm. widersetzen*
reveller	*Feiernder*
revenge	*Rache*
reverberate back	*zurückprallen*
reward	*Belohnung*
riddle	*Rätsel*
ridge	*Bergzug, Buckel*
rightful	*rechtmäßig*
rim	*Rand*
robbed of any credibility it may have had	*jeder Glaubwürdigkeit beraubt, die sie angeblich jemals besaß*
roll one's eyes	*die Augen verdrehen*
rough	*grob*
rule	*herrschen*
ruler	*Herrscher*
rumbling	*grollend*
rump	*Hinterteil*
sacrificed	*geopfert*
saddle	*Sattel*
saddle a horse	*ein Pferd satteln*
say sth. out loud	*etw. laut sagen*
scale	*Schuppe*
scattered	*zerstreut, versprengt*
scornful	*spöttisch*
scoundrels and cheats	*Schwindler und Schlitzohren*
scrabbling	*Scharren*
scrubland	*Buschland*
seal	*besiegeln*
send sb. flying	*jdn. zum Boden schleudern*
set up camp	*ein Lager aufschlagen*
sew up	*zuschnüren*
shadow	*Schatten, Schemen*
shadowy	*schattig*
shaft	*Schaft*
shake off	*abschütteln*
shaky	*zitternd*
shaman	*Schamane*
she beckons him to sit next to her	*sie macht eine einladende Geste neben sich*
She cannot hide the fact that…	*Sie kann nicht mehr verhehlen, dass…*

She only just reaches his chin.	*Sie reicht ihm gerade bis zum Kinn.*
sheath a sword	*sein Schwert einstecken*
sheer	*schier*
shelter	*Obdach, Unterschlupf*
shimmer	*schimmern*
shining white	*strahlend weiß*
shortcut	*Schleichweg*
shove	*Stoß*
shrill	*schrill*
shrink	*schrumpfen*
shrug one's shoulders	*mit den Achseln zucken*
shying	*scheuend*
side with sb.	*sich auf jds. Seite stellen*
sigh	*seufzen*
size sb. up	*jdn. kritisch mustern*
skilfully	*geschickt*
skull	*Schädel*
sleek	*schmal; glatt*
sleeveless	*ärmellos*
slender	*schmal*
slightly slurred	*leicht lallend*
slip around	*hin- und herrutschen*
slip out	*sich davonstehlen*
slit sb.'s throat	*jdm. die Kehle durchschneiden*
slope	*Böschung*
smirk	*höhnisch grinsen*
snap	*fauchen; schnappen*
snatch sth. from sb.'s hand	*jdm. etw. aus der Hand reißen*
sneering	*spöttisch*
sniff sb.	*jdn. beschnüffeln*
snore away	*vor sich hin schnarchen*
snort	*schnauben*
solid	*fest*
Something bad might happen to me…	*Mir könnte etwas Schlimmes zustoßen…*
soothing	*beruhigend, tröstend*
sound out	*erschallen*
source of power	*Kraftquelle*
spare	*entbehren, erübrigen, verschonen*
spear on a stick	*auf einem Stock spießen*
spill sth.	*etw. verschütten*
spit fire	*Feuer speien*
splash	*spritzen*
sprinkle	*träufeln*
squeak	*Quieken*
stabbing	*stechend*
stable a horse	*ein Pferd unterbringen*
stain	*beflecken, besudeln*
stand a chance	*eine Chance haben*
stand face-to-face with sb.	*jdm. gegenüberstehen*
stand guard	*wachen*
stand with sb.	*jdm. beisstehen*
start at sth.	*wegen etw. zusammenfahren*
start out	*sich auf den Weg machen*
starve	*hungern*
state of mind	*Geisteszustand*
steady	*fest*
steep	*steil, abschüssig*
steeper than it looks	*steiler, als es den Anschein hatte*
stir	*sich regen*
stoke	*anfachen*
stomach sth.	*etw. verkraften*

straggly	*struppig*
strangely enough	*komischerweise*
stream through sb.	*jdn. durchströmen*
strengthen one's character	*den Charakter stählen*
string	*Sehne*
struggling to control oneself	*mühsam beherrscht*
stumble	*stolpern*
suffer	*leiden, erleiden*
suffocate	*ersticken*
summit	*Gipfel, Bergkuppe*
summon up	*aufbringen, zusammennehmen*
supplies	*Proviant*
supposed to sound like...	*sollten klingen wie...*
suspicion	*Verdacht*
swampy	*sumpfig*
swear	*schwören*
sweep	*fegen*
swig	*Schluck*
take a fall	*stürzen*
take care of sb.	*auf jdn. Acht geben*
take turns doing sth.	*etw. abwechselnd machen*
tangible	*greifbar*
task	*Aufgabe*
temple	*Schläfe*
tense	*angespannt*
tense up	*sich spannen*
terrain	*Boden, Gelände*
that he does not even have time to shout in surprise	*dass ihm nicht einmal mehr Zeit für einen überraschten Schrei bleibt*
That is the way it is. (Redewendung)	*So ist es.*
That will be the end of you.	*Dann ist es um dich geschehen.*
the best thing that's ever happened to sb.	*das Beste, was jemandem jemals widerfahren ist*
the fate that awaited her	*das Schicksal, das sie erwartete*
the huge flatness of the plains	*die weiten, flachen Ebenen*
the latter	*Letzteres*
the least likely	*am Unwahrscheinlichsten*
the odd bit of torture	*ein bisschen Folter hin und wieder*
the slow slur of his speech	*seine schleppende Art zu sprechen*
the sublime	*das Erhabene*
the worst of the cold	*die ärgste Kälte*
then again	*andererseits*
There can be no going back. (Redewendung)	*Es gibt kein Zurück mehr.*
There is nothing for you to be ashamed of	*Es gibt nichts, was du dir vorzuwerfen hättest*
thief	*Dieb*
thigh	*Schenkel*
think better of sth.	*sich eines Besseren besinnen*
thoughtfully	*nachdenklich*
thrive	*gedeihen*
throw one's arms around sb.'s neck	*jdm. um den Hals fallen*
thud into sth.	*in etw. dumpf einschlagen*
tightly-closed eyelids	*zusammengepresste Augenlider*
torso	*Oberkörper*
torture sb.	*jdn. quälen*
torturer	*Folterknecht*

touched	*gerührt, bewegt*
tower	*emporstreben*
tracker	*Spurenleser*
trail	*schleifen*
trail	*Spur*
traitor	*Verräter*
treachery	*Verrat*
tremble	*schütteln, beben*
tribesmen	*Stammesmänner*
trot	*traben*
trust sb.	*jdm. vertrauen*
turn down sth.	*ablehnen*
turn one's back on sb.	*sich von jdm. abwenden*
twilight	*Zwielicht*
twitch	*zucken*
two wrongs do not make a right	*zweimal falsch ergibt nicht einmal richtig*
uncertainty	*Unsicherheit*
unchecked	*unbeirrt, unbeeindruckt, ungehemmt, ungehindert*
uncomfortable	*unbehaglich*
unconcerned	*sorglos*
unconsciousness	*Bewusstlosigkeit*
undisguised mistrust	*unverhohlenes Misstrauen*
unearthly	*unheimlich*
unfortunate	*misslich, unglücklich*
uninhibited	*unbeherrscht, hemmungslos*
unjust	*unfair*
unprotected	*ungeschützt*
unsettled	*verunsichert*
untouched	*unberührt*
urgent	*dringend*
utter confusion	*völlige Fassungslosigkeit*
utter sth. (altertümlich)	*etw. sprechen*
vein	*Ader, Vene*
very moving speech	*herzergreifende Rede*
voice a word	*ein Wort verlieren*
vow	*Schwur*
wade	*waten*
walking stick	*Wanderstab*
weigh two things up against one another	*zwei Sachen gegeneinander abwiegen*
weird	*merkwürdig, unheimlich*
well rested	*ausgeruht*
well up	*aufkommen, aufwallen*
What show-offs these Tajin are!	*Sie sind furchtbare Angeber, diese Tajin!*
What is that supposed to prove?	*Was soll das beweisen?*
What nonsense is this?	*Was redest du für einen Unsinn?*
What of it? (altertümlich)	*Na und?*
what will become of it	*was daraus werden wird*
whatever it takes	*koste es, was es wolle*
wheeze	*keuchen*
when he is confronted with someone stronger	*wenn er einem Stärkeren gegenübersteht*
when humans had not even been thought of	*als man an Menschen noch nicht einmal dachte; als der Mensch noch nicht einmal eine Idee war*
Where are you headed to?	*Wohin seid ihr jetzt unterwegs?*

whisper	*flüstern*
white-hot	*weißglühend*
who has a better understanding of such matters	*der sich besser darauf versteht*
whom they can turn	*an die sie sich wenden können*
wicked	*niederträchtig*
wide-eyed with disbelief	*mit ungläubig aufgerissenen Augen*
willpower	*Willenskraft*
wily	*verschlagen, gerissen*
winded	*atemlos, nach Atem ringend*
wink	*zwinkern*
wintry	*winterlich*
wipe	*wischen*
wipe out	*auslöschen*
wisdom	*Weisheit*
wit	*Witz*
with his sword drawn	*mit gezogenem Schwert*
with no respite	*ununterbrochen, ohne Pause*
without flinching	*ohne mit der Wimper zu zucken; ohne die Miene zu verziehen*
without real conviction	*ohne Überzeugung*
wooden	*hölzern*
worthwhile	*der Mühe wert*
wound	*Wunde*
wounded	*verletzt*
wrist	*Handgelenk*
yank	*reißen, zerren*
yoke	*Joch*
You mark my word (Redewendung)	*mein Wort darauf*
yurt	*Jurte (Zelt)*

Aufgaben

Forced to Flee

1. Snow and ice

Timucin, Arbesa und Üdschin sind auf der Flucht vor den Tajin. Dabei ist das Wetter der allgegenwärtige Feind, der ihnen das Leben erschwert. Verbinde diese englischen Begriffe, die das Wetter beschreiben, mit den passenden deutschen Übersetzungen.

1. snowflake
2. frozen
3. flurry
4. snowdrift
5. chilling

a) Gestöber
b) Schneeflocke
c) gefroren
d) beißend
e) Schneewehe

2. Fleeing

In diesem Kapitel lernen wir, dass Timucin mitsamt Anhang schon seit einiger Zeit auf der Flucht ist. Wie heißt aber „auf der Flucht" auf English: *in the run, at the run* oder *on the run*? Und wie wird das Verb *to run* sonst oft übersetzt?

Es ist leichter, Vokabeln, die inhaltlich zusammen gehören, auch zusammen zu lernen. Du kannst noch weitere Wörter im Wörterbuch oder unter www.pons.eu suchen und zum Beispiel zu deiner Liste „Winter" hinzufügen.

A Familiar Face

3. The dragon

Timucin begegnet Sarantuya ja nur in seiner Traumwelt: Und bei der Übermittlung dieses Textausschnittes aus ihrer Drachendimension sind einige Wörter durcheinandergebracht worden. Kannst du die kryptischen Anagramme entschlüsseln?

As a child, he (1) lievbeed ________ that the dragon was real, made of flesh and (2) ldoob ________ and shimmering armoured scales and invisible for some reason or other. Later, he realised that Sarantuya does exist, in a way, but that she exists in (3) ernotha ________ world. This world is as real as his world, but far, far away – further away than the mountains behind the (4) orhizno ________.

4. An old friend

Unerwartet läuft Timucin ein alter Freund über den Weg: Arbesa ist misstrauisch und fürchtet, Chuzir sei im Dienste des Feindes. Überprüfe die folgenden Sätze auf ihre Richtigkeit und entscheide selber, ob sich ihr Misstrauen mit Tatsachen begründen lässt.

	richtig	falsch
1. Chuzir and Timucin have a swordfight before recognising each other.	☐	☐
2. Chuzir could slit Timucin's throat, but does not.	☐	☐
3. Chuzir refuses to call Timucin "Khan" because he has been defeated.	☐	☐
4. Chuzir creeps up on the group so that they do not hear him coming.	☐	☐
5. Chuzir leaves again immediately, saying he has to get his horse.	☐	☐

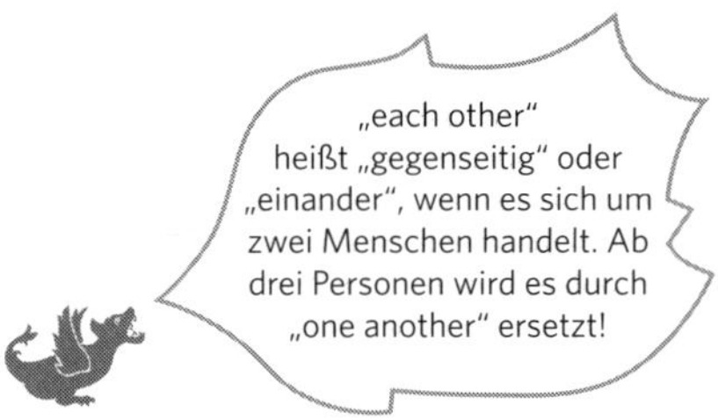

Friend or Foe?

5. The improvised feast

Ihr Wiedersehen feiern Timucin und Chuzir mit einem improvisierten Festmahl, bestehend aus den wenigen dürftigen Zutaten, die sie noch haben. Verbinde die Beschreibungen dieses Gelages mit den richtigen Vokabeln.

1. Aykol, the alcoholic drink Chuzir enjoys, is made from this.
2. After killing Üdschin's pony, they have lots of this.
3. Instead of glass bottles, they use these to carry aykol.
4. This word describes meat cooked on an open fire.

a) pouches ______

b) mare's milk ______

c) roast meat ______

d) horsemeat ______

Übersetze nun diese Begriffe ins Deutsche!

6. Tribal rebellion

Nach dem Essen besprechen die vier Kijat wie es dazu kam, dass sich der Klan um Timucin auflöste. Sie benutzen dabei einige Wörter, die mit Stämmen und Stammespolitik zu tun haben. Unbemerkt liegt im Schnee eine Schlange und schnappt sich diese Vokabeln auf: kannst du diese finden?

Was heißt nun das letzte Wort in der Schlange auf Deutsch? Und welches andere Wort in der Schlange kann man anwenden, um dies zu beschreiben?

______

______

The Holy Mountain

7. A hard climb

Timucin nimmt sich vor, den Heiligen Berg Burchan Chaldun zu besteigen: kein leichtes Unterfangen, wie sich herausstellt. Du hast es wesentlich besser, denn du musst nur die passenden Begriffe in die Lücken setzen, um den Text zu vervollständigen!

1. At first, the climb appears easy, but the mountain is ______ than it looks.
2. The final ______ is very hard; when he reaches the ______, Timucin is exhausted.
3. At the summit of the mountain, the air is ______ and Timucin has trouble breathing.
4. On the ______ down the mountain, Timucin has to find paths round the ______ cliff faces.

steeper thin peak ascent sheer descent

8. Seeing into the future

Auf dem Berg enthüllt Sarantuya dem kleinen Timucin seine große Zukunft: Aus ihm wird der berühmte Dschingis Khan werden! Dabei muss sich der Drache natürlich der Zukunftsform mit will bedienen, die man ja bei Vorhersagen einsetzt. Kannst du Sarantuya dabei helfen?
Achtung: Einen Satz musst du auch noch verneinen.

You (1) ______ be called Genghis Khan, the greatest ruler of your people and founder of a huge empire. People (2) ______ speak your name with respect and awe; but although you (3) ______ spend the rest of your life on the run, soon you (4) ______ go through a time of pain and suffering.

Vergiss nicht, dass die Verneinung der Zukunftsform sehr oft verkürzt wird: aus *I will not* wird in der Umgangssprache *I won't*. In formellen Texten wird es oft aber noch vollständig ausgeschrieben.

Betrayal

9. Timucin flees

In diesem Kapitel kommen einige Wortstämme doppelt vor – einmal als Substantiv und einmal als Verb (also wie „Sturz" und „stürzen" auf Deutsch). In dieser Übung musst du entweder das Substantiv oder das Verb durch ihren Gegenpart ergänzen.

Substantiv	Verb
betrayal	to ....
....	to fall
....	to pursue
plea	to ....
....	to flee

10. Who will he save?

In diesem Kapitel muss Timucin ständig Pferde hinter sich herzerren oder Menschen auf Pferde heraufholen. Dabei kommen einige englische Begriffe für das Ziehen und Zerren von Menschen und Gegenständen vor. Aber welches der Wörter hat nichts damit zu tun?

to yank | to pull | to slap | to drag | to draw

Und was bedeutet der eine Begriff, der nicht in der Reihe passt?

....

The Broken Oath

11. At the Tajin's mercy

Timucin ist in die Gefangenschaft der Tajin geraten und muss ein Joch tragen. Er wird belästigt, bedroht und gefoltert. Einige Wörter, die dabei vorkommen, findest du unten hinter Gittern – rette sie da heraus! Die Wörter können senkrecht, waagrecht und quer stehen. Ein paar Begriffe werden so gefoltert, dass sie sogar rückwärts laufen müssen.

H	E	T	H	R	E	A	T	E	N
P	U	N	C	H	E	J	S	K	S
E	A	M	C	V	D	E	N	A	S
C	N	I	I	A	C	B	I	R	T
N	I	O	N	L	K	I	A	T	O
E	R	F	B	R	I	M	H	E	R
L	A	E	U	G	N	A	C	F	F
O	E	I	F	B	R	U	T	A	L
I	N	E	A	U	T	Y	X	E	U
V	S	G	E	D	A	R	G	E	D

Captivity

12. Khan of the Pigs

Um Timucin seinen Platz in der Hackordnung unmissverständlich zu bedeuten, ketten ihn die Tajin im Schweinepferch an. Im schlammigen Boden des Pferches sind nun einige Begriffe aus diesem Absatz verloren gegangen. Kannst du den richtigen Ersatz auswählen?

Two pigs come over to sniff their new (1) pen friend / penmate / pencil , and Timucin waits until they are close enough before (2) kicking / punching / slapping the bigger of the two animals in its curious, sniffing nose. He probably hasn't even (3) hurt / damaged / fought the animal, but the kick was hard enough for the pig to run away with a (4) afraid / alarmed / frightened squeak; the second animal follows.

> Nicht vergessen:
> Vor einem Vokal oder einem lautlosen Konsonanten wird *a* zu *an* – also *a pig* aber *an ugly pig*. Du wirst schnell ein Gefühl dafür entwickeln, wo du *an* brauchst, weil es den Sprachfluss erleichtert!

13. Strangely enough…

In diesem Kapitel denkt Timucin darüber danach, dass die Tajin ihn jederzeit töten könnten, doch komischerweise hat er kaum Angst davor. Komischerweise auf Englisch heißt *strangely enough*: bring diese weiteren Begriffe, die aus einem Adverb und *enough* bestehen, mit der richtigen deutschen Übersetzung zusammen.

1. luckily enough	a) überraschenderweise
2. oddly enough	b) enttäuschenderweise
3. disappointingly enough	c) seltsamerweise
4. surprisingly enough	d) glücklicherweise

Flight

14. Reviewing the situation

In diesem Kapitel muss Timucin überlegen, ob er erneut die Flucht ergreifen soll oder nicht. Die englische Vokabel für dieses Abwägen und Entscheiden findest du hier in Anagrammform, also mit vertauschten Buchstaben, wieder. Entschlüssle die Anagramme und ordne dann das Ergebnis der passenden Übersetzung zu.

1.	DREISONC	C________	a) sich entscheiden
2.	EGHIW PU	W________U____	b) überdenken
3.	CIDEDE	D________	c) abwägen
4.	OSHOEC	C________	d) überlegen
5.	INKHT VORE	T________O____	e) wählen

15. Successful escape?

Timucin wird auf der Flucht von seinem Wächter im Fluss gefunden und versucht ihn so lange mit Fragen aufzuhalten, bis der richtige Moment kommt, ihn zu überfallen. Die Wörter, die er braucht, um Fragen zu stellen, fließen unten im Strom: Greif die heraus und füll damit die Lücken!

1. ________ you want to kill me now?
2. What ________ I tell him you helped me escape?
3. How ________ he know that you are not lying?
4. ________ you should have a look in your yurt first...
5. ________ will you explain this to your Khan?

how do perhaps will if

The Fight

16. Sarantuya's message

Nun ist Timucin Kesrit entkommen und er unterhält sich mit Sarantuya, die ihm erklärt, warum sie ihn bei den Tajins so lange hat warten lassen: Er hat gelernt, sich der Anliegen Unterdrückter anzunehmen. Finde die Wörter, die sie dabei benutzt.

Welches von diesen Wörtern heißt *gedeihen* auf Deutsch?

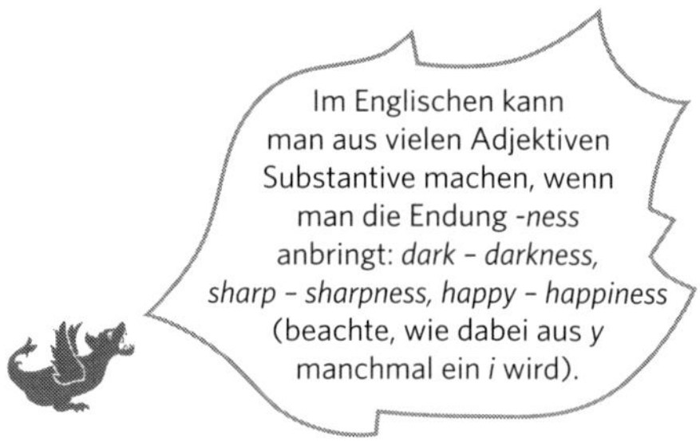

17. Seeing and staring

Im Englischen werden Verben oft mit Präpositionen verknüpft, um ihre Bedeutung zu ändern. In diesem Text gibt es einige Stellen, wo du entscheiden muss, ob noch eine benötigt wird oder nicht: Füll die Lücke mit der richtigen Präposition oder lass sie leer.

Timucin tries to look (1) ______ Sarantuya, but cannot see (2) ______ her. Chuzir is staring (3) ______ Timucin.

In the pen, Timucin looks (4) ______ like a real prisoner, which pleases Kesrit as he eyes (5) ______ him.

Timucin cannot see (6) ______ the warriors, but he tries to look (7) ______ them.

A Friend

18. Are you awake?

Nachdem er das Joch zerschlagen hat und Kesrit getötet worden ist, wird Timucin ohnmächtig. Das englische Wort dafür ist: unconscious. Einmal die Aussprache gemeistert, kann man daraus viele neue Wörter ableiten – wie die unten, die du vervollständigen und mit der passenden deutschen Übersetzung in Verbindung bringen musst.

1. consciousn___s	a) Bewusstlosigkeit
2. su___onscious	b) modebewusst
3. unconscious___	c) teilweise unbewusst
4. s___i-conscious	d) Bewusstsein
5. f___hio___-conscious	e) unterbewusst

19. Safe at last?

Timucin ist nun sehr schwach und muss sich ganz auf seinen Schwurbruder Chuzir verlassen: Diesmal wird Chuzir ihn nicht verraten. Dennoch hat Timucin einen Moment Angst, dass er dies doch tun könnte. Wenn du die Sätze unten aber auf ihre Richtigkeit prüfst, dann wirst du Timucin beruhigen können.

	richtig	falsch
1. Chuzir has shot Kesrit and stopped him killing Timucin.	☐	☐
2. Timucin punches Chuzir in the ribs to defend himself.	☐	☐
3. Chuzir leaves and returns with Tajin solidiers who imprison Timucin.	☐	☐
4. When Chuzir comes back with soldiers, Timucin is scared.	☐	☐
5. Chuzir offers his life to Timucin to apologise for what he did.	☐	☐

20. Genghis Khan

Timucin spares Chuzir's life and does not want revenge. In fact, he asks Chuzir to make them a new arrow of friendship to renew their oath. Why could this be surprising now that we know that Timucin will become the famous Genghis Khan?

21. Arrow word puzzle

Löse dieses Kreuzworträtsel mit Vokabeln aus der ganzen Geschichte und stelle für Timucin und Chuzir einen neuen Freundschaftspfeil her!

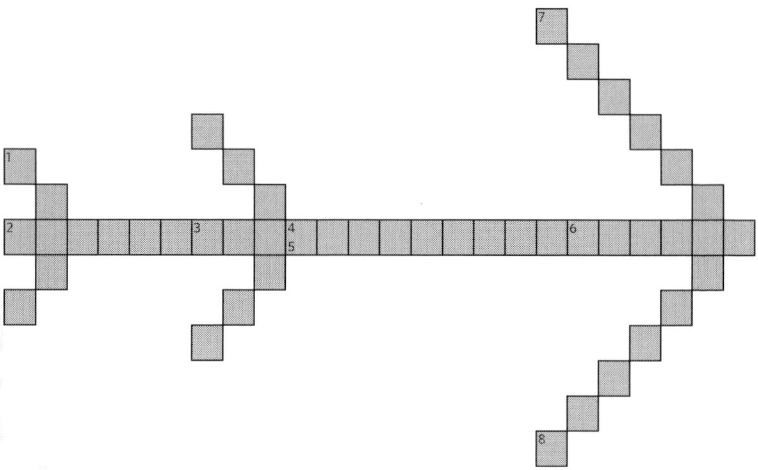

1. Pferd (bogenförmig von oben nach unten)
2. Drache
3. Heiliger Berg
4. Jurte (rückwärts nach oben)
5. Joch (rückwärts nach unten)
6. Ehre
7. Krieger
8. Verräter

Lösungen

Forced to Flee

1. Snow and ice

1-b, 2-c, 3-a, 4-e, 5-d

2. Fleeing

on the run. *Run* bedeutet rennen oder laufen.

A Familiar Face

3. The dragon

1) believed, 2) blood, 3) another, 4) horizon

4. An old friend

1-f, 2-r, 3-f, 4-r, 5-r

Friend or Foe

5. The improvised feast

1-b Stutenmilch, 2-d Pferdefleisch, 3-a Trinkbeutel, 4-c gebratenes Fleisch

6. Tribal rebellion

loyal, tribe, leader, honour, oath, allies. Das letzte Wort, *allies*, bedeutet Verbündete. Man kann auch *loyal allies* sagen.

The Holy Mountain

7. A hard climb

1) steeper, 2) ascent, peak, 3) thin, 4) descent, sheer

8. Seeing into the future

1) will be called, 2) will speak, 3) will not spend, 4) will go through

Betrayal

9. Timucin flees

betrayal – to betray
fall – to fall
pursuer / pursuit – to pursue
plea – to plead
flight – to flee

10. Who will he save?

to yank – zerren
to pull – ziehen
to drag – schleppen, schleifen, ziehen
to draw – ziehen
Nicht in die Reihe gehört: to slap, das heißt schlagen oder klatschen.

The Broken Oath

11. At the Tajin's mercy

humiliated, degrade, punch, cangue, brutal, violence, pain, threaten

H	E	T	H	R	E	A	T	E	N
P	U	N	C	H	E	J	S	K	S
E	A	M	C	V	D	E	N	A	S
C	N	I	I	A	C	B	I	R	T
N	I	O	N	L	K	I	A	T	O
E	R	F	B	R	I	M	H	E	R
L	A	E	U	G	N	A	C	F	F
O	E	I	F	B	R	U	T	A	L
I	N	E	A	U	T	Y	X	E	U
V	S	G	E	D	A	R	G	E	D

Captivity

12. Khan of the Pigs

1 - penmate, 2 - kicking, 3 - hurt, 4 - frightened

13. Strangely enough...

1-d, 2-c, 3-b, 4-a

Flight

14. Reviewing the situation

1 - consider - d, 2 - weigh up - c, 3 - decide - a, 4 - choose - e, 5 - think over - b

15. Successful escape?

1 - do, 2 - if, 3 - will, 4 - perhaps, 5 - how

The Fight

16. Sarantuya's message

starve, spare, diplomat, thrive, fate, suffering. To thrive bedeutet gedeihen.

17. Seeing and staring

(1) at, (3) at, (7) for

A Friend

18. Consciousness

1 - consciousness - d,
2 - subconscious - e,
3 - unconsciousness - a,
4 - semi-conscious - c,
5 - fashion-conscious - b

19. Safe at last?

1 - r, 2 - f, 3 - f, 4 - r, 5 - r

20. Genghis Khan

Timucin's act of forgiveness for his old friend is surprising to people who have read about Genghis Khan, because Genghis Khan is known to many as a brutal ruler who took revenge against enemies by killing their entire tribes.
Dass Timucin seinem alten Freund verzeiht, könnte viele Menschen überraschen, die schon etwas über Dschinghis Khan gelesen haben. Denn er ist vielen als brutaler Herrscher bekannt, der sich an Feinden rächte, indem er ihre Stämme gänzlich auslöschte.

21. Arrow word puzzle

1. horse, 2. dragon, 3. holy mountain, 4. yurt, 5. yoke, 6. honour, 7. warrior, 8. traitor

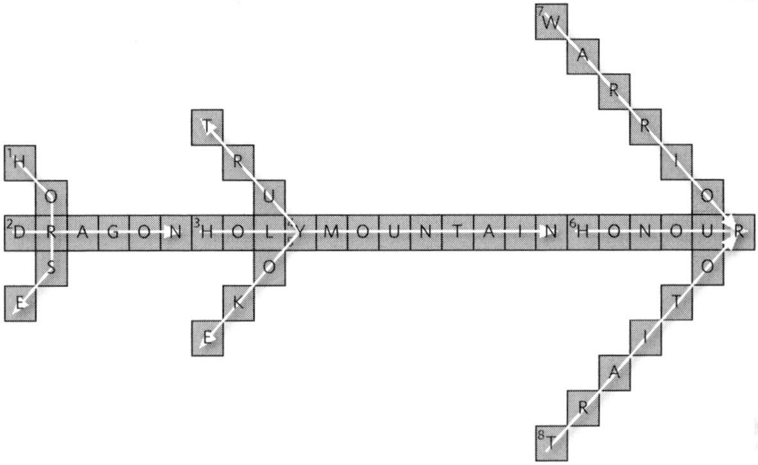
1 H O R S E
2 D R A G O N
3 H O L Y M O U N T A I N
T R U L O K E
6 H O N O U R
7 W A R R I O R
8 T R A I T O R

Drachenfragen und -antworten

Forced to Flee

Where does Timucin tell his mother and Arbesa that they are fleeing to?

Timucin erzählt seiner Mutter und seiner Verlobten, dass sie auf der Flucht zum heiligen Berg Burchan Chaldun sind und dort Hilfe suchen.

A Familiar Face

Why is an insult made to Chuzir also an insult to Timucin?

Weil die beiden Schwurbrüder sind. Das heißt, dass sie einen Eid geschworen haben, sich gegenseitig zu schützen – jeder Angriff auf den einen ist also auch ein Angriff auf den anderen.

Friend or Foe?

Why, in Üdschin's opinion, was it so easy for Tedschen to turn the Kijats against Timucin?

Üdschins Meinung nach war Timucin nicht nur zu jung und unerfahren, um sich gegen die Männer des Stammes durchzusetzen. Hinzu kam, dass sie selbst von ihrem Mann von einem fremden Stamm in den Stamm der Kijat gebracht und deswegen von vielen abgelehnt wurde – ebenso ihr Sohn Timucin, der aufgrund der Herkunft seiner Mutter als Bastard bezeichnet wird.

The Holy Mountain

Timucin meets Sarantuya again in this chapter. What is different about the way she looks and sounds?

Timucin sieht Sarantuya zum ersten Mal im wirklichen Leben, wo sie ihn doch früher immer im Traum besucht oder ihn in seinen Gedanken angesprochen hat. Ihre Stimme ist nun viel lauter und sie ist unglaublich groß.

Betrayal

In this chapter, Timucin has to decide whether to save Arbesa or his mother – and chooses his mother Üdschin. Is she happy about his decision?

Üdschin ist wütend, weil Timucin seine Verlobte den Tajin überlässt und damit Schande auf sich selbst und seinen Stamm lädt. Sie ist der Meinung, er hätte lieber sie, Üdschin, opfern sollen.

The Broken Oath

Why did Chuzir, who swore an oath to protect Timucin, feel forced to betray him?

Die Tajin hatten seine Familie als Geisel genommen und hätten diese getötet, hätte er sich geweigert, Timucin, seine Mutter und Arbesa preiszugeben. Deswegen muss Chuzir seinen Eid, Timucin zu schützen, brechen.

Captivity

Why does Tedschen not kill Timucin as soon as he has been captured?

Beim erzwungenen Verrat von Timucin macht es Chuzir zu Bedingung, dass Timucin nicht sofort getötet werden darf. Tedschen muss schwören, Timucin erst dann im fairen Einzelkampf zu töten, wenn dieser das Mannesalter erreicht hat.

Flight

Why is this the last chance that Timucin will have to escape from his captivity?

Weil er bald das Mannesalter erreichen und Tedschen ihn dann töten wird. Außerdem wird es keine bessere Gelegenheit geben, weil sich die Krieger an diesem Abend maßlos bet[illegible]n und tief schlafen w[illegible]en

[illegible]

How does Timucin escape the yoke?

Timucin schlägt das Joch gegen eine Felswand, bis es zerbricht – und er zusammenbricht.

A Friend

Why does Chuzir break the arrow of friendship?

Weil Chuzir sich dafür schämt, dass er Timucin an die Tajin ausliefern musste, zerbricht er den Freundschaftspfeil und bietet seinem Schwurbruder seinen Dolch an, damit er ihn tötet, um diese Schande wieder gutzumachen

Noch mehr Englisch mit Wolfgang Hohlbein

AGE OF DRAGONS

Faszinierende Drachenabenteuer

Timucin hat keinen leichten Stand im Klan. Die anderen Jungkrieger machen ihm das Leben schwer, denn im Bogenschießen und im Schwertkampf ist er nur Mittelmaß. Zudem hat er panische Angst vor Hunden, obwohl der Hund doch der engste Freund eines jeden Kriegers ist! Sogar Timucins Schwurbruder Chuzir fällt ihm in den Rücken und verbündet sich mit seinen Gegnern.
Doch Timucin hat ein besonderes Geheimnis: Nachts bekommt er Besuch von einem rätselhaften Drachen. Dann lernt er die stolze Arbesa kennen – und muss sich schließlich der schwersten aller Prüfungen stellen.

Ab dem 3. Lernjahr

Format: 13,5 x 19,5 cm, 128 Seiten.
Broschur mit MP3-CD.
ISBN: 978-3-12-010070-6

PONS
www.pons.de